THE IMITATION OF
CHRIST

THOMAS À KEMPIS

THE IMITATION OF CHRIST

TRANSLATED AND
WITH AN INTRODUCTION BY
LEO SHERLEY-PRICE

DORSET PRESS
New York

This translation first published 1952

This edition published by Dorset Press,
a division of Marboro Books Corporation,
by arrangement with Penguin Books Ltd.
1986 Dorset Press

Distributed in the United Kingdom by Bibliophile Editions

ISBN 0-88029-078-1
(Formerly ISBN 0-14-044-027-5)

Printed in the United States of America
M 9 8 7 6 5

CONTENTS

CONTENTS

CONTENTS

CONTENTS

THE CHAPTERS OF THE FOURTH BOOK

On the Blessed Sacrament

CONTENTS

INTRODUCTION

THE CHARACTER OF THE *IMITATION*

It would be impossible to estimate the wide and profound influence that this wonderful little book has exercised throughout Christendom for over five hundred years. After the Bible itself, |no other work can compare with its profound wisdom, clarity of thought, and converting power. Christians of such widely differing period and outlook as S. Thomas More and General Gordon, S. Ignatius Loyola and John Wesley, S. Francis Xavier and Dr Johnson, are but a few of the thousands who have acknowledged their debt to this golden work.

It may perhaps appear strange that a book written by one who spent nearly the whole of his long life in the cloister, and who intended his works primarily for his fellow-religious, should have such power to guide and inspire hundreds who have little knowledge of monastic life: but the writer's deep and burning love of God, his deep humility, his profound knowledge of the Scriptures and the writings of the Fathers, coupled with his understanding of human nature and its needs, make him a wise and trustworthy counsellor to all who seek to know and fulfil the true purpose of human life – 'to praise, love and serve God their Lord, and by doing these things, to save their souls'.[1] Accordingly, while Thomas à Kempis writes in the first place for his fellow-religious, an ascetic for ascetics, a mystic for those who aspire to mystical union with God through the evangelical counsels of poverty, chastity, and obedience, yet his counsels are a proved guide and inspiration to men and women of every age and nation.

The secret of the amazing influence and converting power of this little book is the secret of the lives of all the Saints – their nearness to God, and the reflection of His love in their lives and writings. Thomas's theme is the love, mercy, and holiness of God; with vivid clarity he shows man's complete dependence on, and need of, God, and the empty futility of life lived apart from its only source of true Life and Light: he stirs us to seek our own good and lasting happiness in the

1. S. Ignatius Loyola *Spiritual Exercises.*

knowledge and service of God. In the words of S. Augustine, Patron of the Order of Canons Regular to which Thomas himself belonged, 'O God, Thou hast made us for Thyself, and our hearts are restless until they rest in Thee.' In simple and burning words, Thomas shows that the only road to this sublime goal of oneness with God is by devotion to Christ Crucified, and by treading his 'Royal Road to the Holy Cross'.[1] Moreover, while the author is both a mystic and a scholar, he is always – like S. Teresa of Avila – eminently realistic and practical, and he shows us the 'how' as well as the 'why' of the spiritual life.

In his authoritative work on à Kempis, the late Dr F. R. Cruise writes: 'Beyond doubt, the Imitation most perfectly reflects the light which Jesus Christ brought down from heaven to earth, and truthfully portrays the highest Christian philosophy. When our divine Saviour preached the Sermon on the Mount, He held up as the characteristics of His followers – perfect humility, poverty of spirit, purity of heart, meekness, sorrow for sin, forgiveness of injustice, and peace and joy in the midst of persecution. Nowhere else do we find these doctrines so incisively and persuasively taught as in this unpretending little volume.'[2]

There is a common tendency today to represent the Saints as experts in 'natural' religion or 'perennial philosophy'; as men and women who, by breaking the chains of Christian dogma, have been enabled by their own natural genius to attain to union with the Divine. Probably the most frequent victim of such misrepresentation is that most loyal son of the Church, S. Francis of Assisi. But in the Imitation, as in the lives of the Saints, will be found sincere and reasoned loyalty to the teachings of Christ and His holy Catholic Church, and Thomas lays emphasis on right belief as the prerequisite of right life. He is no nature-mystic, nor would he regard as worthy of serious consideration many modern attempts to ignore the true nature of man, or to produce a synthesis of Christian and pagan philosophies as a guide to the spiritual life. For Thomas, as for all Christians, the sole road to God is through the power and teachings of Jesus Christ, true God and true Man; by the subordination of nature to divine

1. *Imitation*, ii, 12.   2. *Thomas à Kempis*, Kegan Paul (London 1887).

grace; by self-discipline; and by devout use of the Sacraments of the Catholic Church, in particular that of the Holy Eucharist.

The modern reader will perhaps find minor portions of the book, such as the chapters on monastic life,[1] inapplicable in detail to his own needs, but they stand as a worthwhile reminder that the fundamental spirit and intention of the Religious Orders is identical with that of all devout Christians, i.e. the following of Christ and the pursuit of perfection. The widespread revival of the Religious Life during the past century, and its call for selfless service to God and man, provides a living witness and effective admonition that the Christian life requires personal discipline and self-sacrifice, coupled with unswerving loyalty to the Person and teachings of Christ our Saviour. The powerful challenge of godless Communism today would make small headway if all those 'who profess and call themselves Christians' were as active and devoted in the following of Christ as are many of their adversaries in the service of anti-Christ. And it is this very devotion to Christ and His Church that Thomas seeks to stimulate.

Commenting on the purpose and nature of the *Imitation*, one writer says: 'The philosophy of the *Imitation* may be summed up in two words. It is a philosophy of Light, and a philosophy of Life:[2] the Light of Truth, and the Life of Grace. Both the one and the other à Kempis seeks as their source and fountain-head. He does not separate them. It is only in the union of both that man attains his philosophic ideal. ... So the Devout author, with Clement of Alexandria and Aquinas, ascends to the Incarnate Word – the divine *Logos* – as the Source whence proceeds all truth, both natural and revealed, for the criterion and ideal of human knowledge. Here he finds unity and harmony ... it is not only the Light of Truth; it is also the Life of Grace. This life consists in the practice of the Christian virtues; the practice of the Christian virtues leads up to union with Christ; and union with Christ is consummated in the Holy Eucharist. Such is the author's philosophy of life, and in its development does his genius especially glow. He is mystical, eloquent, sublime. He soars into the highest regions of truth, in which meet both poetry and philosophy. Following in the footsteps of Christ, heeding His words, living in intimate union with Him, loving Him with a love that counts no

1. i, 17-20.   2. See *Imitation*, iii, 23.

sacrifice too great, trampling underfoot all things displeasing to Him, bearing one's burden cheerfully for His sake – such is the life of the soul as revealed in this wonderful book.'[1]

Thomas à Kempis is not only a master of the spiritual life, he is a master writer as well; consequently we have in the *Imitation* a classic that richly repays careful study and re-reading. As with the Scriptures, the more familiar we are with this book, the fairer the riches we discover in its pages, and the more it becomes a part of ourselves. Open it where one will; on every page will be found something to instruct, to inspire, to give ample food for thought.

It is hardly surprising that a man of Thomas's spiritual and mental powers was widely and soundly read in the best both of pagan and Christian literature. Every page glows with the reflected light of holy Scripture, which he knows so intimately; but he loves also to draw from the wisdom of the Christian Fathers, and from the great philosophers of Greece and Rome, in order to confirm and illustrate his teaching. Anyone familiar with the writings of S. Bernard, S. Augustine, and S. Thomas Aquinas can readily detect the thought of these great theologians, while Thomas also draws from Ovid, Seneca, and Aristotle. Like the householder of the Gospels, 'he brings out of his treasure things new and old',[2] to illustrate the great truths of God, man, and life.

OUTLOOK OF THE BOOK

BOOK ONE: *Counsels on the Spiritual Life*

Here Thomas seeks firstly to wean the soul from preoccupation with solely material interests, successes and failures, and from dependence on its fellows, and to set before it the Christian teaching on life, on human nature, and on its essential need of God. He shows how, by winning control of our passions, and by overcoming conceit and complacency, we may, like S. Paul, become spiritual athletes, and enter upon the way of purgation, which is the first stage of the soul's

1. *The Culture of the Spiritual Sense*, by Bro. Azarias. (Steigel & Co., New York, 1884).
2. Matt. xiii, 52.

progress towards its divinely appointed destiny of union with God. Sincere self-knowledge will bring the soul to a realization of its own nothingness and need of God. The humble following of Christ, and the power of His grace alone can transform our lives, 'for if you rely on your own reasoning and ability rather than on the transforming power of Jesus Christ, you will seldom and only slowly attain wisdom. For God wills that we become perfectly obedient to Him, and that we rise above cold reason on the wings of a burning love for Him.'[1] The Book continues with counsels addressed primarily to Religious, but which are also of value to all who pursue perfection. It concludes by urging the disciple to complete the good work of purgation now begun and sets before him considerations on true contrition, on man's last end, on God's judgement of sinners and man's need of amendment.

BOOK TWO : *On the Inner Life*

This sets forth the second stage of the spiritual life – the way of illumination – in which the disciple, having made some progress in self-conquest, is gradually illumined by the divine light of the knowledge of God. Here Thomas sets forth the Christian standards of value, spiritual and material: we are shown how the spiritual and eternal is to be prized above the material and transitory, 'for men soon change, but Christ abides for ever, and stands firmly by you to the end' (Ch. 1). Through purity of heart and simplicity of purpose, man is raised and cleansed (Ch. 4); and by self-knowledge he is freed from the temptation to pass judgement on others (Ch. 5). The book continues, to speak of the wonders of the love of Jesus, and the glory of His friendship, that only His loved ones know (Chs. 7, 8): and shows that the only road to this desired consummation is that which Jesus Himself has revealed, the road of the Cross, so meaningless to the world, so powerful to the faithful pilgrim. Many fear to tread this hard road (Ch. 11), which is the sole road to God. Yet 'See, how in the Cross all things rest, and how in dying upon it all things depend. There is no other way to life and true inner peace than the way of the Cross, and of daily self-denial: ... our merit and spiritual progress do not consist in enjoying great delight and consolation, but rather in the

1. *Imit.* i, 14.

bearing of great burdens and troubles' (Ch. 12). But the love of Jesus
will amply outweigh all sacrifices, and light the steep upward path.

BOOK THREE : *On Inward Consolation*

In the third and longest book, Christ calls on the disciple to seek Him
alone, and shows him the way of union and true peace. Aware of the
perils that beset the steep ascent of the Mount of God, and seeing all
things in their true light, the disciple is led to choose God as his true
and only goal (Ch. 3). He is shown how, by the light of grace, he can
gradually win free from the entanglements of the world, the flesh, and
the devil, and come freely to Christ. In response, the disciple sings the
joys and glories of the love of God, and prays: 'Deepen Your love in
me, O Lord, that I may learn in my inmost heart how sweet it is to
love, to be dissolved, and to plunge myself into Your love. Let Your
love possess me, and raise me above myself with a fervour and wonder
above all imagination. Let me sing the song of love. Let me follow
You, my Beloved, into the heights. Let my soul spend itself in Your
praise, rejoicing for love. ...' (Ch. 5). There follow chapters of
practical counsels on the Christian life: on the gradual conquest of
self; on the divine virtues of love, obedience, patience, humility, and
trust, which must be cultivated as the soul advances with God's help
on the road towards perfection (Chs. 7–15). We are shown how
holiness is not to be sought as an end in itself, but that we must rest in
God alone above all other good, 'above all health and beauty, above
all glory and honour, above all power and dignity, above all joy and
gladness . . . and above all that is not Yourself, O my God' (Ch. 21).
Christ then reveals (Ch. 23) four ways to obtain freedom and peace of
spirit, 'the whole secret of perfection', and the disciple offers a most
beautiful prayer for mental light. He is then shown (Ch. 25) how the
true source of peace and progress rest 'in complete surrender of the
heart to the will of God, not seeking to have one's own way either in
great matters or small, in time or eternity'. Freedom of mind is not to
be achieved by study so much as by prayer and direct contact with the
Source of all light and life (Ch. 26). In the ensuing chapters the disciple
is warned that obedience to Christ does not imply that he will be
freed from sorrow, distraction, or temptation: rather will the Devil

redouble his efforts to deter the spiritual athlete, who can expect no ease in this life, but is comforted by the assurance of final victory through perseverance and faith. 'Wait for the Lord: fight manfully and with high courage. Do not despair, do not desert your post; steadfastly devote yourself, body and soul, to the glory of God. I will give you a rich reward, and will be with you in all your troubles' (Ch. 35). The disciple cannot rely on his fellow men for help; God alone can order his affairs aright, and bring good out of ill. He must therefore fix his heart and mind on God in all and above all, as did the holy martyr Agatha, who cried, 'My mind is firmly established and grounded in Christ' (Ch. 45). The disciple is next shown how no evils that the ingenuity of the Devil or man can inflict have power to do real injury to the soul who trusts and lives wholly in Christ (Chs. 46, 47), and who looks steadfastly towards its heavenly home. Nor is the disciple to be overmuch concerned with success or failure, honour or dishonour; 'Let this be your constant desire, that whether in life or death, God may at all times be glorified in you' (Ch. 50). The only way to overcome the corruption of human nature is by self-discipline, that the power of grace may have full play in us; 'for grace is a supernatural light, and the especial gift of God, the seal of His chosen, and the pledge of salvation, that raises man from earthly things to love the heavenly, and from being worldly, makes him spiritual. Therefore the more nature is controlled, the richer the graces bestowed' (Ch. 55). The Third Book concludes by urging the disciple to banish all discouragement (Ch. 57); to cultivate humility (Ch. 58); to avoid controversy; and to place his entire trust in God; 'for where You are, there is Heaven; and where You are not, there is Death and Hell. . . . You alone are the End of all good things, the fullness of life, and the depth of wisdom; and the greatest comfort of Your servants is to trust in You above all else' (Ch. 59).

BOOK FOUR: *On the Blessed Sacrament*

This begins with 'A devout exhortation to Holy Communion', but does far more than encourage the faithful to regular and devout Communion. It deals also with the theological and historical background of the Eucharist, and shows this sacred rite to be the central sun around which all the worship and sacraments of the Church revolve. Here Thomas, true to the doctrine and experience of the Church, shows this sublime Sacrament to be both the effectual pleading of the sacrifice of Christ's death on the Cross, and the fulfilment of His last loving command at the Last Supper, and also the covenanted means of grace and unique act of Christian worship. In this Sacrament the Christian knows Christ Himself to be truly and actually present, hiding His glory beneath the simple forms of bread and wine. Here Christ pleads His sacrifice before the eternal Father: here His Church lifts up holy hands in sacrifice and intercession; here Christ feeds the faithful with His very Self, Body, Blood, Soul and Divinity. The altar is the vital link between God and man, heaven and earth, where angels and men join in adoration of the crucified and risen Christ.

Thomas therefore begins by emphasizing the simple and direct invitation of Christ to the faithful, who desire to have part in Him. He shows the prophetic nature of the ancient sacrifices of the Law, and the need of even greater devotion towards the Sacrament of Christ than that so amply displayed by the great kings and prophets towards the Ark, the Temple, and the sacrifices of old: 'for how great a difference is there between the Ark of the Covenant with its relics, and Your most holy Body with its ineffable powers; between the sacrifices of the old Law that foreshadowed the Sacrifice to come, and the true Victim of Your Body, which fulfils all the ancient rites' (Ch. 1). The generosity, goodness, and condescension of God are richly shown in this Sacrament (Ch. 2), which is to be regularly and devoutly received, with a deep sense of unworthiness (Ch. 3). In Chapter 4, the disciple acknowledges his unworthiness, and prays for the transforming graces of this Sacrament. Chapter 5 is addressed in particular to priests, as guardians and dispensers of the Most Holy Sacrament, and calls on them to couple the supreme privilege and dignity of the priesthood with the highest possible standard of life and devotion, since 'a priest should be adorned with all virtues, and show an example of holy life to others . . . for when a priest celebrates the Eucharist, he honours God and gives joy to the Angels; he edifies the Church, aids the living, obtains rest for the departed, and makes himself a sharer in all good things.' Chapters 6 and 7 deal with preparation

for Communion, which should include careful self-examination,
confession, and sincere purpose of amendment. In Chapters 8 and 9,
Christ calls on the disciple for complete surrender to the will of God:
'Naked I hung on the Cross with arms outstretched, offering Myself
freely to God the Father for your sins, My whole Person a sacrifice to
appease divine displeasure: you, also, must willingly offer yourself
daily to Me in the Eucharist, with all your powers and affections as a
pure and holy offering. . . . I do not seek your gifts, but yourself.' The
disciple responds to this plea, asking pardon for his sins, and praying
for the needs of the faithful: 'I offer to You whatever is good in me
though it be little and imperfect, that You may strengthen and hallow
it, make it dear and acceptable to You, and raise it continually towards
perfection.' Christ then warns the disciple (Ch. 10) against the temptation to regard Holy Communion as reserved for the holy, since it is
the fountain of grace and mercy for penitent sinners. In Chapters 11
and 12, the disciple speaks of his insatiable longing for God alone
above all His gifts and graces, and for Christ as his heavenly food. I
acknowledge my need of two things – food and light. You have
therefore given me in my weakness Your sacred Body as the refreshment of my soul and body, and have set Your Word as a light to my
feet. Without these two, I cannot rightly live; for the Word of God
is the light of my soul, and Your Sacrament is the Breath of my life.'
The disciple is filled with longing for Christ his Beloved (Ch. 13); he
recalls the boundless love shown by other devout souls towards
Christ in His Sacrament (Ch. 14); and grieves at the inadequacy of
his love as compared with theirs. In Chapter 15, Christ reveals how
this grace of devotion can be won by humility and self-denial, and is
the gift of God alone. The disciple then makes renewed acts of love
and desire for Christ (Ch. 16); and recalling the glorious lives of the
Saints, cries (Ch. 17): 'Although I am not fit to enjoy such feelings of
devotion as they, yet I offer You all the love in my heart . . . and whatever a pious heart can conceive or desire, that I offer You with all
reverence and love.' The Book concludes with Christ warning the
disciple against 'curious and unprofitable inquiries' into the manner of
His Presence in this Sacrament, since 'God can do more than man can
comprehend'. The requirements of God are 'faith and a holy life'. 'All
reason and research must follow faith, but not precede or encroach

upon it. For in this most holy and excellent Sacrament, faith and love precede all else, working in ways unknowable to man.'

THE LIFE OF THOMAS À KEMPIS

Since a book is the offspring of an author's mind, it will be of value to learn a little about this master of the spiritual life, whose devotion and experience are reflected in the pages of the *Imitation*.

Thomas à Kempis, so called from his birthplace at Kempen, near Düsseldorf, was born of humble parents, John and Gertrude Haemerken, of whom little is known, and whose claim to fame rests in their two sons, John (born 1365) and Thomas (born 1380), both of whom were destined to become distinguished sons of the Church, the former as Prior of Agnetenburg (Mount S. Agnes), and the latter as the illustrious author of the *Imitation* and many other works.

Devoutly brought up by his mother, and educated at Kempen Grammar School, Thomas left home at the early age of thirteen to join his elder brother at Deventer, where John had attached himself to the Congregation of the Common Life, a brotherhood founded by the great Gerard Groote, and approved by Pope Gregory XI in 1376. It will be necessary to make a digression here, in order to give a brief account of Gerard, whose foundation was to have so great an influence on Thomas, and whose biography he was later to write.

Gerard Groote was born at Deventer in 1340 of wealthy parents, and early showed great talents. Entering the University of Paris at the age of fifteen, he took high degrees, and subsequently received several rich preferments that allowed him to indulge his natural taste for influence and luxury. This brilliant man was not, however, to remain long satisfied with worldly honours, and influenced by Henry Calcar, Prior of the Carthusians at Monichuisen, Gerard was moved to resign all his lucrative offices, and retired with his friend to Monichuisen in order to re-orientate his whole life and outlook, and to seek God's guidance as to his future work. He remained here for three years, employed in constant prayer, study, and self-discipline; then, with the unanimous approval of the Community, he set out to evangelize the country. Such was the appeal of this brilliant Christian orator that thousands were moved to amend their lives, and Gerard's mission greatly prospered; but its very success roused the anger and jealousy of lax and unworthy clergy, who by false charges at length persuaded the Bishop of Utrecht to suspend Gerard from preaching. Unjust as was the sentence, Gerard humbly accepted it, and turned his zealous energy to writing, and to advising individuals and communities who sought his help. Settling once more at Deventer, his magnetic personality drew a number of priests and laymen around him, and the nucleus of an informal religious community was formed. This society was not bound by permanent vows, but its members lived together under a Rule in poverty, chastity, and obedience, holding all things in common, and earning their own livelihood. Its object was to challenge the laxity and corruption of the times by a return to apostolic zeal and simplicity. 'They were of one heart and mind in God,' Thomas was to write later; 'what each possessed was held in common, and being content with plain food and clothing, they took no thought for the morrow.' Among these disciples of Gerard Groote was Florentius Radewyn, who from its earliest days played a leading part in the development of a regular Community, and whom Gerard appointed to succeed him at his death.

Influenced by the holiness of John Ruysbroeck, Prior of the Augustinian Canons Regular at Groenendaal, Gerard determined to place his Congregation under its direction and Rule; but his death of the plague in 1384 prevented this, and it was left to Florentius to carry out the founder's wishes. With the consent of the Bishop of Utrecht, a site for a monastery was chosen at Windesheim, near Zwolle, in 1386, and it was in this Community that Thomas was to spend most of his long life.

To return to Thomas à Kempis, he remained at Deventer under the guidance of Florentius for seven years, during which time he acquired a great regard for this holy priest, and the devotion which he taught. 'Never before do I remember to have seen men so devout, so full of love for God and their fellow-men. Living in the world, they were altogether unworldly,' says Thomas of Florentius and his companions. In 1399, with the approval of Florentius, Thomas travelled to Zwolle, and sought admission to the new monastery of Mount S. Agnes, where his brother John had become Prior. Here began his long life in Religion; here he learned to obey the words of his Master, 'If any man will come after Me, let him deny himself, and take up his cross, and follow Me.' Thomas made his profession in 1406, and received the priesthood in 1413 at the age of thirty-three. It was probably during the years immediately preceding and following his ordination that he compiled the four books of the *Imitation*.

During his long life as a Canon of S. Augustine, Thomas spent much time in the copying of the Scriptures and altar books for the use of the House, and, in addition to his masterpiece, wrote many other works in which his learning and devotion are almost equally reflected, but which are less well known today: *Prayers and Meditations on the Life of Christ, Sermons to Novices, Spiritual Exercises, The Elevation of the Mind, The Soliloquy of the Soul, The Garden of Roses, On True Compunction of Heart, On Solitude and Silence, On the Discipline of the Cloister*, and several biographies, including those of Gerard Groote and Florentius Radewyn. He is said to have been an eloquent preacher, and a wise confessor. Modest and retiring both by nature and conviction, Thomas sought no office or fame; as he mentions in his *Exercises*, silence was his friend, work his companion, and prayer his aid, and he was well content to work unknown.

Of Thomas's outwardly uneventful life, little remains to be told. In 1425 he was elected Sub-Prior, and acted as Master of Novices; he also kept the Chronicle of the monastery. His main work ever remained that of all good Religious – the cultivation of the spiritual life, and the personal following of Christ; his achievement in this life-work, known in its entirety to God alone, is reflected in the wide influence and converting power of his *Imitation*.

In the spring of 1471, Thomas's long and useful life drew to its close. In the words of his successor as Chronicler of Mount S. Agnes: 'In the same year, on the Feast of S. James the Less (1 May), after Compline, our Brother Thomas Haemerken, born at Kempen, a town in the diocese of Cologne, departed from this earth. He was in the 92nd year of his age, the 63rd of his religious clothing, and the 58th of his priesthood. In his youth, he was a disciple, at Deventer, of Master Florentius, who sent him to his own brother, who was then Prior of Mount S. Agnes. Thomas, who was then 20 years of age, received the habit from his brother at the close of six years' probation, and from the outset of his monastic life he endured great poverty, temptations, and labours. He copied out our Bible and various other books, some of which were used by the convent, and others were sold. Further, for the instruction of the young, he wrote various little treatises in a plain and simple style, which in reality were great and important works, both in doctrine and efficacy for good. He had an especial devotion to the Passion of Our Lord, and understood admirably how to comfort those afflicted by interior trials and temptations. Finally, having reached a ripe old age, he was afflicted with dropsy of the limbs, slept in the Lord in the year 1471, and was buried in the east side of the cloister, by the side of Peter Hebort.'

The monastery of Mount S. Agnes was destroyed in the troubles of the sixteenth century (1573), and its very site almost obliterated. In 1672, however, the Elector of Cologne ordered a search for Thomas's tomb, which was subsequently discovered and indisputably authenticated. His remains were placed in a casket, and after resting for two hundred years in the chapel of S. Joseph, were transferred to the Church of S. Michael in Zwolle, where they remain to this day.

THE AUTHORSHIP OF THE *IMITATION*

This has for a long time been in dispute, but an Introduction is not the place to attempt to set forth the lengthy and abstruse arguments put forward by opponents of Thomas's authorship, nor would much interest or profit result from such an attempt. Happily, the importance and value of this golden book in no way depend on its authorship, but on its contents, since no other book of Christian devotion has ever exercised such unbroken and world-wide influence for good as the *Imitation*. We may therefore do well to follow the advice of the author, when he says: 'Do not be influenced by the importance of the writer, and whether his learning be great or small; but let the love of pure truth draw you to read. Do not inquire, "Who said this?" but pay attention to what is said.'[1]

Without, therefore, entering into historical or textual details of this question, to which scholars have devoted much time and research, we may state briefly that, at one time or another, the following claimants to the authorship of the *Imitation* have been advanced: Jean Charlier

I. i, 5.

Gerson, Chancellor of Paris; Gerard Groote; S. Bernard of Clairvaux; S. Bonaventura; Henry de Calcar; Landolph of Saxony; Walter Hilton; and others. Exhaustive research has effectively disposed of the claims of all these, with the doubtful exception of Gerard Groote, the case for whose (partial) authorship has been ably argued by the Rev. Joseph Malaise, s.j., of San Francisco, in his translation of parts of the *Imitation*, which he describes as 'The Spiritual Diary of Gerard Groote' (1937). In the view of the present translator, the case which he presents with considerable skill is entirely inconclusive, and it seems evident that, while Thomas was well acquainted with the thought and writings of Groote (whose biography he wrote), and that all Thomas's writings reflect the characteristic devotion and ethos of the 'Circle of Windesheim', yet all the evidence points as clearly to the authorship of Thomas for the *Imitation* as it does to the remainder of his writings.

The case for Thomas's authorship may be summarized as follows:

1. *Internal evidence.* The style, thought, and phraseology of the *Imitation* are those found in Thomas's other works, as also is his frequent indirect quotation of the writings of S. Bernard, S. Augustine and S. Thomas Aquinas, all of whom he particularly revered.

2. *External evidence.* No MS of the *Imitation* has been found which dates from earlier than Thomas's middle age (when Groote had been dead fifty years), while the well-known Brussels autograph MS (1441), contains thirteen spiritual treatises by Thomas, and including the four 'books' of the *Imitation*, closes with the note: 'Finitus et completus anno Domini MCCCCXLI, per manus Fratris Thome Kempis in Monte Sanctae Agnetis prope Zwollis.' 'Finished and completed by the hand of Brother Thomas à Kempis in the year 1441, at the Monastery of Mount S. Agnes near Zwolle.' It is hardly conceivable that the humble Thomas would have included among his own works one which – in view of the high repute of Groote – was well known to be not his own, but that of Groote.

3. *The evidence of contemporary witnesses.* These include members of Thomas's own community at Mount S. Agnes, who are unanimous in making specific mention of Thomas's authorship of the *Imitation*. Of many, three may be mentioned: John Busch, Thomas's successor as Chronicler of Windesheim (1400–79); Herman Ryd (1408–?), who speaks of Thomas being alive at the time of writing; and Wessel

24

Gansford, who mentions that he visited Mount S. Agnes with the particular purpose of meeting the author of the *Imitation*.

The majority will probably be agreed that there is little reasonable doubt of Thomas's authorship, the uncertainty over which may well have arisen in the first place through his own modesty and reticence, since the *Imitation* first became known without specific mention of his authorship. But since the truth was well known and testified to by members of his own Community both during his life and subsequently, it is the translator's view that Thomas's authorship is well nigh indisputable.

Earlier Translations. The first translation into English (from French) was in 1503, when the Fourth Book was translated by Margaret, Countess of Richmond, mother of Henry VII, and printed by Richard Pynson, the King's Printer. This was followed the same year by a translation of the first three Books by William Atkinson, D.D. In 1556, a complete translation was made by Richard Whytford, a member of the Augustinian Canons of Syon House, London, and author of the well-known *Jesus Psalter*. This long remained the best and standard translation.

Since those early days, a number of translations have appeared, but many suffer from incompleteness or obscurity of style. Firstly, translators have taken considerable liberties with Thomas's text, making unacknowledged omissions and alterations of the original whenever their personal views did not agree with those of the author. Secondly, even the more recent translations have been rendered in pseudo-Jacobean English, which make them unnecessarily involved for the modern reader, and obscure the direct, vibrant phrases of the original Latin. Therefore, while it is not possible to reproduce the effect of Thomas's 'rhythmic' Latin style in modern prose, I have attempted to retain something of its simplicity and directness. My purpose in attempting a completely new version is to provide an accurate, unabridged, and readable modern translation, and thus to introduce this spiritual classic to a wider public. If this is achieved, I am confident that many a new reader of the *Imitation* will come to treasure this little book, and read it again year by year.

Leo Sherley-Price

BOOK ONE

COUNSELS ON THE
SPIRITUAL LIFE

CHAPTER I
On the Imitation of Christ

'HE who follows Me shall not walk in darkness,' says Our Lord.[1]

In these words Christ counsels us to follow His life and way if we desire true enlightenment and freedom from all blindness of heart.[2] Let the life of Jesus Christ, then, be our first consideration.

The teaching of Jesus far transcends all the teachings of the Saints, and whosoever has His spirit will discover concealed in it heavenly manna.[3] But many people, although they often hear the Gospel, feel little desire to follow it, because they lack the spirit of Christ.[4] Whoever desires to understand and take delight in the words of Christ must strive to conform his whole life to Him.

Of what use is it to discourse learnedly on the Trinity, if you lack humility and therefore displease the Trinity? Lofty words do not make a man just or holy; but a good life makes him dear to God. I would far rather feel contrition than be able to define it. If you knew the whole Bible by heart, and all the teachings of the philosophers, how would this help you without the grace and love of God? 'Vanity of vanities, and all is vanity,'[5] except to love God and serve Him alone.[6] And this is

1. John viii, 12.   3. Rev. ii, 17.   5. Eccles. i, 2.
2. Mark iii, 5   4. Rom. viii, 9.   6. Deut. vi, 13.

supreme wisdom – to despise the world, and draw daily nearer the kingdom of heaven.

It is vanity to solicit honours, or to raise oneself to high station. It is vanity to be a slave to bodily desires,[1] and to crave for things which bring certain retribution. It is vanity to wish for long life, if you care little for a good life. It is vanity to give thought only to this present life, and to care nothing for the life to come. It is vanity to love things that so swiftly pass away, and not to hasten onwards to that place where everlasting joy abides.

Keep constantly in mind the saying, 'The eye is not satisfied with seeing, nor the ear filled with hearing.'[2] Strive to withdraw your heart from the love of visible things, and direct your affections to things invisible. For those who follow only their natural inclinations defile their conscience, and lose the grace of God.

CHAPTER 2
On Personal Humility

EVERYONE naturally desires knowledge,[3] but of what use is knowledge itself without the fear of God? A humble countryman who serves God is more pleasing to Him than a conceited intellectual who knows the course of the stars, but neglects his own soul.[4] A man who truly knows himself realizes his own worthlessness, and takes no pleasure in the praises of men. Did I possess all knowledge in the world, but had no love,[5] how would this help me before God, who will judge me by my deeds?

Restrain an inordinate desire for knowledge, in which is found much anxiety and deception. Learned men always wish

1. Gal. v, 16.   3. Aristotle, *Metaphy-*   4. Ecclus. xix, 22.
2. Eccles. i, 8.   *sics*, I, 1.   5. 1 Cor. xiii, 2.

to appear so, and desire recognition of their wisdom. But there are many matters, knowledge of which brings little or no advantage to the soul. Indeed, a man is unwise if he occupies himself with any things save those that further his salvation. A spate of words does nothing to satisfy the soul, but a good life refreshes the mind, and a clean conscience[1] brings great confidence in God.

The more complete and excellent your knowledge, the more severe will be God's judgement on you, unless your life be the more holy. Therefore, do not be conceited of any skill or knowledge you may possess, but respect the knowledge that is entrusted to you. If it seems to you that you know a great deal and have wide experience in many fields, yet remember that there are many matters of which you are ignorant. So do not be conceited,[2] but confess your ignorance. Why do you wish to esteem yourself above others, when there are many who are wiser and more perfect in the Law of God? If you desire to know or learn anything to your advantage, then take delight in being unknown and unregarded.

A true understanding and humble estimate of oneself is the highest and most valuable of all lessons. To take no account of oneself, but always to think well and highly of others is the highest wisdom and perfection. Should you see another person openly doing evil, or carrying out a wicked purpose, do not on that account consider yourself better than him, for you cannot tell how long you will remain in a state of grace. We are all frail; consider none more frail than yourself.

1. 1 Tim. iii, 9.   2. Rom. xi, 20.

CHAPTER 3

On the Teaching of Truth

HAPPY the man who is instructed by Truth itself, not by signs and passing words,[1] but as It is in itself. Our own conjectures and observations often mislead us, and we discover little. Of what value are lengthy controversies on deep and obscure matters, when it is not by our knowledge of such things that we shall at length be judged? It is supreme folly to neglect things that are useful and vital, and deliberately turn to curious and harmful things. Truly, 'we have eyes and see not'[2]: for what concern to us are such things as *genera* and *species*?

Those to whom the Eternal Word speaks are delivered from uncertainty. From one Word proceed all things,[3] and all things tell of Him; it is He, the Author of all things, who speaks to us.[4] Without Him no one can understand or judge aright. But the man to whom all things are one, who refers everything to One, and who sees everything as in One, is enabled to remain steadfast in heart, and abide at peace with God.

O God, living Truth,[5] unite me to Yourself in everlasting love![6] Often I am wearied by all I read and hear. In You alone is all that I desire and long for. Therefore let all teachers keep silence, and let all creation be still before You; do You, O Lord, speak alone.

The more closely a man is united to You in pure simplicity, the more varied and profound the matters which he understands without effort, for he receives light and understanding from heaven. A pure, simple, and stable man, however busy and occupied, does not become distracted thereby, for he does

1. Num. xii, 8. 3. John i, 3. 5. John xiv, 6.
2. Jer. v, 21; John xii, 4. John viii, 25. 6. Jer. xxxi, 3.
40; Rom. xi, 8.

all things to the glory of God, and strives to preserve himself free from all self-seeking. And what harms and hinders you more than the undisciplined passions of your own heart? A good and devout man firstly sets in order in his mind whatever tasks he has in hand, and never allows them to lead him into occasions of sin, but humbly subjects them to the dictates of a sound judgement. Who has a fiercer struggle than he who strives to conquer himself?[1] Yet this must be our chief concern – to conquer self, and by daily growing stronger than self, to advance in holiness.

All perfection in this life is accompanied by a measure of imperfection, and all our knowledge contains an element of obscurity. A humble knowledge of oneself is a surer road to God than a deep searching of the sciences. Yet learning itself is not to be blamed, nor is the simple knowledge of anything whatsoever to be despised, for true learning is good in itself and ordained by God; but a good conscience and a holy life are always to be preferred. But because many are more eager to acquire much learning than to live well, they often go astray, and bear little or no fruit. If only such people were as diligent in the uprooting of vices and the planting of virtues as they are in the debating of problems, there would not be so many evils and scandals among the people, nor such laxity in communities. At the Day of Judgement, we shall not be asked what we have read, but what we have done; not how eloquently we have spoken, but how holily we have lived. Tell me, where are now all those Masters and Doctors whom you knew so well in their lifetime in the full flower of their learning? Other men now sit in their seats, and they are hardly ever called to mind. In their lifetime they seemed of great account, but now no one speaks of them.

Oh, how swiftly the glory of the world passes away![2] If only the lives of these men had been as admirable as their learning,

1. Wisd. x, 12.   2. 1 John ii, 17

their study and reading would have been to good purpose! But how many in this world care little for the service of God, and perish in their vain learning. Because they choose to be great rather than humble, they perish in their own conceit.[1] He is truly great, who is great in the love of God. He is truly great, who is humble in mind, and regards earth's highest honours as nothing. He is truly wise who counts all earthly things as dung, in order that he may win Christ.[2] And he is truly learned, who renounces his own will for the will of God.

CHAPTER 4
On Prudence in Action

WE should not believe every word[3] and suggestion, but should carefully and unhurriedly consider all things in accordance with the will of God. For such is the weakness of human nature, alas, that evil is often more readily believed and spoken of another than good. But perfect men do not easily believe every tale that is told them, for they know that man's nature is prone to evil,[4] and his words to deception.[5]

It is wise not to be over hasty in action, nor to cling stubbornly to our own opinions. It is wise also not to believe all that we hear, nor to hasten to report to others what we hear or believe. Take counsel of a wise and conscientious man, and seek[6] to be guided by one who is better than yourself, rather than to follow your own opinions. A good life makes a man wise towards God, and gives him experience in many things.[7] The more humble and obedient to God a man is, the more wise and at peace he will be in all that he does.

1. Rom. i, 21.
2. Phil. iii, 8.
3. Ecclus. xix, 16.
4. Gen. viii, 21.
5. Ecclus. xiv, 1.
6. Tobit iv, 19.
7. Ecclus. xxxiv, 9.

CHAPTER 5

On Reading the Holy Scriptures

In the holy Scriptures, truth is to be looked for rather than fair phrases. All sacred scriptures should be read in the spirit in which they were written. In them, therefore, we should seek food for our souls rather than subtleties of speech, and we should as readily read simple and devout books as those that are lofty and profound. Do not be influenced by the importance of the writer, and whether his learning be great or small, but let the love of pure truth draw you to read. Do not inquire, 'Who said this?'[1] but pay attention to what is said.[2]

Men pass away, but the word of the Lord endures for ever.[3]

God speaks to us in different ways,[4] and is no respecter of persons.[5] But curiosity often hinders us in the reading of the Scriptures, for we try to examine and dispute over matters that we should pass over and accept in simplicity. If you desire to profit, read with humility, simplicity, and faith, and have no concern to appear learned. Ask questions freely, and listen in silence to the words of the Saints; hear with patience the parables of the fathers, for they are not told without good cause.

CHAPTER 6

On Control of the Desires

Whenever a man desires anything inordinately, at once he becomes restless. A proud and avaricious man is never at rest; but a poor and humble man enjoys the riches of peace. A man who is not yet perfectly dead to self is easily tempted, and is

1. Seneca, *Epist.* XII.   3. Ps. cxvii, 2.   5. Ecclus. vi, 35; viii,
2. S. Augustine, on Ps.   4. Col. iii, 25.   9.
xxxvi.

33

overcome even in small and trifling things. And he who is
weak in spirit, and still a prey to the senses and bodily passions,
can only with great difficulty free himself from worldly lusts.
Therefore he is sad when he does so withdraw himself, and is
quickly angered when anyone opposes him. Yet, if he obtains
what he desires, his conscience is at once stricken by remorse,
because he has yielded to his passion, which in no way helps
him in his search for peace. True peace of heart can be found
only by resisting the passions, not by yielding to them. There
is no peace in the heart of a worldly man, who is entirely
given to outward affairs; but only in a fervent, spiritual man.

CHAPTER 7
On Avoiding Vain Hope and Conceit

WHOEVER puts his confidence in men or in any creature is
very foolish. Do not be ashamed to be the servant of others for
love of Jesus Christ, and to appear poor in this world. Do not
trust in yourself, but put your whole confidence in God. Do
what you are able, and God will bless your good intention.
Do not trust in your own knowledge, nor in the cleverness of
any man living, but rather in the grace of God, who aids the
humble,[1] and humbles the proud.

Do not boast of your possessions, if you have any, nor of the
influence of your friends; but glory in God,[2] who gives all
things and desires above all things to give you Himself. Do
not be vain about your beauty or strength of body, which a
little sickness can mar and disfigure. Take no pleasure in your
own ability and cleverness, lest you offend God, who has
Himself bestowed on you all your natural gifts.

Do not esteem yourself better than others, lest you appear
worse in the eyes of God, who alone knows the heart of man.[3]

1. James iv, 6.   2. 2 Cor. x, 17.   3. Ps. xciv, 11; John ii, 25.

Do not be proud of your good deeds, for God does not judge as men; and what delights men often displeases God. If you have any good qualities, remember that others have more; and so remain humble. It does you no harm when you esteem all others better than yourself, but it does you great harm when you esteem yourself above others. True peace dwells only in the heart of the humble: but the heart of the proud is ever full of pride and jealousy.

CHAPTER 8

On Guarding against Familiarity

Do not open your heart to everyone,[1] but ask counsel of one who is wise and fears God. Be seldom with young people and strangers. Do not flatter the wealthy, and avoid the society of the great. Associate rather with the humble and simple, the devout, and the virtuous, and converse with them on such things as edify. Avoid undue familiarity with the other sex, but commend all good women to God. Desire to be familiar only with God and his angels, and do not seek the acquaintance of men.

We must live in charity with all men, but familiarity with them is not desirable. It sometimes happens that someone personally unknown to us enjoys a high reputation, but that when we meet him, we are not impressed. Similarly, we sometimes imagine that our company is pleasing, when in reality we offend others by our ill behaviour.

1. Ecclus. viii, 19.

CHAPTER 9
On Obedience and Discipline

IT is an excellent thing to live under obedience to a superior, and not to be one's own master. It is much safer to obey than to rule. Many live under obedience more of necessity than of love, and such people are often discontented and complaining. They will never attain freedom of mind unless they submit with their whole heart for the love of God. Go where you please, but nowhere will you find rest except in humble obedience under the rule of a superior. Preference for other places and desire for change have unsettled many.

Everyone gladly does whatever he most likes, and likes best those who think as he does; but if God is to dwell among us, we must sometimes yield our own opinion for the sake of peace. Who is so wise that he knows all things? So do not place too much reliance on the rightness of your own views, but be ready to consider the views of others. If your opinion is sound, and you forego it for the love of God and follow that of another, you will win great merit. I have often heard that it is safer to accept advice than to give it. It may even come about that each of two opinions is good; but to refuse to come to an agreement with others when reason or occasion demand it, is a sign of pride and obstinacy.

CHAPTER 10
On Avoiding Talkativeness

AVOID public gatherings as much as possible, for the discussion of worldly affairs becomes a great hindrance, even though it be with the best of intentions, for we are quickly corrupted and ensnared by vanity. Often I wish I had remained silent,

36

and had not been among men. But why is it that we are so ready to chatter and gossip with each other, when we so seldom return to silence without some injury to our conscience? The reason why we are so fond of talking with each other is that we think to find consolation in this manner, and to refresh a heart wearied with many cares. And we prefer to speak and think of those things which we like and desire, or of those which we dislike. Alas, however, all this is often to no purpose, for this outward consolation is no small obstacle to inner and divine consolation.

We must watch and pray,[1] that our time may not be spent fruitlessly. When it is right and proper to speak, speak to edify.[2] Evil habits and neglect of spiritual progress are the main cause of our failure to guard the tongue.[3] But devout conversation on spiritual matters greatly furthers our spiritual progress, especially with those who are heart and soul with us in the service of God.[4]

CHAPTER II

On Peace, and Spiritual Progress

WE could enjoy much peace if we did not busy ourselves with what other people say and do, for this is no concern of ours. How can anyone remain long at peace who meddles in other people's affairs; who seeks occasion to gad about, and who makes little or no attempt at recollection? Blessed are the single-hearted,[5] for they shall enjoy much peace.[6]

How were some of the Saints so perfect and contemplative? It is because they strove with all their might to mortify in themselves all wordly desires, and could thus cling to God in their inmost heart, and offer themselves freely and wholly to

1. Matt. xxvi, 41.   3. James iii, 5.   5. Matt. v, 8.
2. Eph. iv, 29.   4. Acts ii, 42.   6. Ps. xxxvii, 11.

37

Him. But we are held too firmly by our passions, and are too much concerned with the passing affairs of the world. We seldom completely master a single fault, and have little zeal for our daily progress; therefore we remain spiritually cold or tepid.

If only we were completely dead to self, and free from inner conflict, we could savour spiritual things, and win experience of heavenly contemplation. But the greatest, and indeed the whole obstacle to our advance is that we are not free from passions and lusts, nor do we strive to follow the perfect way of the Saints. But when we encounter even a little trouble, we are quickly discouraged, and turn to human comfort.

If we strove to stand firm in the struggle like men of valour, we should not fail to experience the help of our Lord from heaven. For He is ever ready to help all who fight, trusting in His grace; He also affords us occasions to fight that we may conquer. If we rely only on the outward observances of religion, our devotion will rapidly wane. But let us lay the axe to the root,[1] that, being cleansed from our passions, we may possess our souls in peace.

If each year we would root out one fault, we should soon become perfect. But, alas, the opposite is often the case, that we were better and purer in the beginning of our conversion than after many years of our profession. Our zeal and virtue should grow daily; but it is now held to be a fine thing if a man retains even a little of his first fervour. If only we would do a little violence to ourselves at first, we would later be enabled to do everything easily and gladly.

It is hard to give up old habits, and harder still to conquer our own wills. But if you cannot overcome in small and easy things, how will you succeed in greater? Resist your evil inclinations in the beginning, and break off evil habits, lest they gradually involve you in greater difficulties. Oh, if you

1. Matt. iii, 10.

could only know how great a peace for yourself and how great a joy for your fellows your good endeavour would win, you would have greater care for your spiritual progress.

CHAPTER 12

On the Uses of Adversity

IT is good for us to encounter troubles and adversities from time to time, for trouble often compels a man to search his own heart. It reminds him that he is an exile here, and that he can put his trust in nothing in this world. It is good, too, that we sometimes suffer opposition, and that men think ill of us and misjudge us, even when we do and mean well. Such things are an aid to humility, and preserve us from pride and vainglory. For we more readily turn to God as our inward witness, when men despise us and think no good of us.

A man should therefore place such complete trust in God, that he has no need of comfort from men. When a good man is troubled, tempted, or vexed by evil thoughts, he comes more clearly than ever to realize his need of God, without whom he can do nothing good. Then, as he grieves and laments his lot, he turns to prayer amid his misfortunes. He is weary of life, and longs for death to release him, that he may be dissolved, and be with Christ.[1] It is then that he knows with certainty that there can be no complete security nor perfect peace in his life.

1. Phil. i, 23.

CHAPTER 13

On Resisting Temptations

So long as we live in this world, we cannot remain without trial and temptation: as Job says, 'Man's life on earth is a warfare.'[1] We must therefore be on guard against temptations, and watchful in prayer,[2] that the Devil find no means of deceiving us; for he never rests, but prowls around seeking whom he may devour.[3] No one is so perfect and holy that he is never tempted, and we can never be secure from temptation.

Although temptations are so troublesome and grievous, yet they are often profitable to us, for by them we are humbled, cleansed, and instructed. All the Saints endured many trials and temptations,[4] and profited by them; but those who could not resist temptations became reprobate, and fell away.[5] There is no Order so holy, nor place so secluded, where there are no troubles and temptations.

No man can be entirely free from temptation so long as he lives; for the source of temptation lies within our own nature, since we are born with an inclination towards evil.[6] When one temptation or trial draws to a close, another takes its place; and we shall always have something to fight, for man has lost the blessing of original happiness. Many try to escape temptations, only to encounter them more fiercely, for no one can win victory by flight alone; it is only by patience and true humility that we can grow stronger than all our foes.

The man who only avoids the outward occasions of evil, but fails to uproot it in himself, will gain little advantage. Indeed, temptations will return upon him the sooner, and he will find himself in a worse state than before. Little by little and by patient endurance[7] you will overcome them by God's

1. Job vii, 1.
2. 1 Peter iv, 7.
3. 1 Peter v, 8.
4. Acts xiv, 22.
5. Ecclus. ix, 11.
6. James i, 14.
7. Col. i, 11.

help, better than by your own violence and importunity. Seek regular advice in temptation, and never deal harshly with those who are tempted, but give them such encouragement as you would value yourself.

The beginning of all evil temptation is an unstable mind and lack of trust in God. Just as a ship without a helm is driven to and fro by the waves, so a careless man, who abandons his proper course, is tempted in countless ways. Fire tempers steel,[1] and temptation the just man. We often do not know what we can bear, but temptation reveals our true nature. We need especially to be on our guard at the very onset of temptation, for then the Enemy may be more easily over-come, if he is not allowed to enter the gates of the mind: he must be repulsed at the threshold, as soon as he knocks. Thus the poet Ovid writes, 'Resist at the beginning; the remedy may come too late.'[2] For first there comes into the mind an evil thought: next, a vivid picture: then delight, and urge to evil, and finally consent. In this way the Enemy gradually gains complete mastery, when he is not resisted at first. And the longer a slothful man delays resistance, the weaker he becomes, and the stronger his enemy grows against him.

Some people undergo their heaviest temptations at the beginning of their conversion; some towards the end of their course; others are greatly troubled all their lives; while there are some whose temptations are but light. This is in accord-ance with the wisdom and justice of God's ordinance, who weighs the condition and merits of every man, and disposes all things for the salvation of those whom He chooses.

We must not despair, therefore, when we are tempted, but earnestly pray God to grant us his help in every need. For, as Saint Paul says, 'With the temptation, God will provide a way to overcome it, that we may be able to bear it.'[3] So, let us

1. Ecclus. xxxi, 26.   2. Ovid, *Remed.*, 91.   3. 1 Cor. x, 13.

humble ourselves under the hand of God[1] in every trial and trouble, for He will save and raise up the humble in spirit.[2] In all these trials, our progress is tested; in them great merit may be secured, and our virtue become evident. It is no great matter if we are devout and fervent when we have no troubles; but if we show patience in adversity, we can make great progress in virtue. Some are spared severe temptations, but are overcome in the lesser ones of every day, in order that they may be humble, and learn not to trust in themselves, but to recognize their frailty.

CHAPTER 14
On Avoiding Rash Judgements

JUDGE yourself, and beware of passing judgement on others. In judging others, we expend our energy to no purpose; we are often mistaken, and easily sin. But if we judge ourselves, our labour is always to our profit. Our judgement is frequently influenced by our personal feelings, and it is very easy to fail in right judgement when we are inspired by private motives. Were God Himself the sole and constant object of our desire, we should not be so easily distressed when our opinions are contradicted.

Very often some inner impulse or outward circumstance draws us to follow it, while many people are always acting in their own interest, although they are not conscious of it. Such appear to enjoy complete tranquillity of mind so long as events accord with their wishes, but at once become distressed and disconsolate when things fall out otherwise. Similarly, differences of opinions and beliefs only too often give rise to quarrels among friends and neighbours, and even between religious and devout people.

1. Judith viii, 17; I Pet. v, 6.   2. Luke i, 52.

Old habits are hard to break, and no one is easily weaned from his own opinions; but if you rely on your own reasoning and ability rather than on the virtue of submission to Jesus Christ,[1] you will but seldom and slowly attain wisdom. For God wills that we become perfectly obedient to Himself, and that we transcend mere reason on the wings of a burning love for Him.

CHAPTER 15

On Deeds Inspired by Love

No motive, even that of affection for anyone, can justify the doing of evil. But to help someone in need, a good work may sometimes be left, or a better undertaken in its place. For in so doing, the good work is not lost, but changed for what is better. Without love, the outward work is of no value; but whatever is done out of love, be it never so little, is wholly fruitful. For God regards the greatness of the love that prompts a man, rather than the greatness of his achievement.

Whoever loves much, does much. Whoever does a thing well, does much. And he does well, who serves the community before his own interests. Often an apparently loving action really springs from worldly motives; for natural inclination, self-will, hope of reward, and our own self-interest will seldom be entirely absent.

Whoever is moved by true and perfect love is never self-seeking, but desires only that God's glory may be served in all things. He envies none, for he seeks no pleasure for himself, nor does he act for self-gratification, but desires above all good things to merit the blessing of God. All good he ascribes not to men, but to God, from whom all things proceed as from their source, and in whom all the Saints enjoy perfection

1. Phil. iii, 21.

and peace. Oh, if only a man had a spark of true love in his heart, he would know for certain that all earthly things are full of vanity.

CHAPTER 16

On Bearing with the Faults of Others

WHATEVER a man is unable to correct in himself or in others, he should bear patiently until God ordains otherwise. Consider, it is perhaps better thus, for the testing of our patience, without which our merits are of little worth. Whenever such obstacles confront you, pray to God that He may grant you His help, and give you grace to endure them in good heart.[1]

If anyone who has been once or twice warned remains obdurate, do not argue with him, but commit all things to God, that His will may be done, and His Name hallowed in all His servants; for He knows well how to bring good out of evil.[2] Strive to be patient; bear with the faults and frailties of others, for you, too, have many faults which others have to bear. If you cannot mould yourself as you would wish, how can you expect other people to be entirely to your liking? For we require other people to be perfect, but do not correct our own faults.

We wish to see others severely reprimanded; yet we are unwilling to be corrected ourselves. We wish to restrict the liberty of others, but are not willing to be denied anything ourselves. We wish others to be bound by rules, yet we will not let ourselves be bound. It is amply evident, therefore, that we seldom consider our neighbour in the same light as ourselves. Yet, if all men were perfect, what should we have to bear with in others for Christ's sake?

Now, God has thus ordered things that we may learn to

1. Matt. vi, 13.   2. Gen. l, 20.

44

bear one another's burdens;[1] for there is no man without his faults, none without his burden.[2] None is sufficient in himself;[3] none is wise in himself;[4] therefore we must support one another,[5] comfort,[6] help, teach, and advise one another. Times of trouble best discover the true worth of a man; they do not weaken him, but show his true nature.

CHAPTER 17

On the Monastic Life

IF you wish to live in peace and harmony with others, you must learn to discipline yourself in many ways. It is not easy to live in a Religious Community and remain there without fault,[7] persevering faithfully until death.[8] Blessed is he who has thus lived happily and well to the end. If you wish to achieve stability and grow in grace, remember always that you are an exile and pilgrim on this earth.[9] Be content to be accounted a fool for Christ's sake[10] if you wish to be a Religious.

The habit and tonsure by themselves are of small significance; it is the transformation of one's way of life and the complete mortification of the passions that make a true Religious. He who seeks in this life anything but God alone and the salvation of his soul will find nothing but trouble and grief.[11] Nor can any remain long at peace who does not strive to be the least[12] and servant of all.[13]

You have come here to serve, not to rule. Remember that you are called to labour and endurance, not to pass your time in idleness and gossip, for in this life men are tried like

1. Gal. vi, 2.
2. Gal. vi, 5.
3. 2 Cor. iii, 5.
4. Prov. iii, 7.
5. Col. iii, 13.

6. 1 Thess. v, 11.
7. Phil. iii, 6.
8. Rev. ii, 10.
9. 1 Pet. ii, 11; Heb. xi, 13.

10. 1 Cor. iv, 10.
11. Ecclus. i, 17; Eccles. i, 18.
12. Luke xxii, 26.
13. 1 Pet. ii, 13.

gold in the furnace.[1] No one can remain here, unless he is ready to humble himself with all his heart for love of God.

CHAPTER 18

On the Examples of the Holy Fathers

CONSIDER the glowing examples of the holy Fathers, in whom shone true religion and perfection; compared with them, we do little or nothing. Alas, how can our life be compared with theirs! The Saints and friends of Christ served Our Lord in hunger and thirst, in cold and nakedness, in toil and weariness: in watching and fasting, in prayer and meditation, in persecutions and insults without number.[2]

How countless and constant were the trials endured by the Apostles, Martyrs, Confessors, Virgins, and all those others who strove to follow in the footsteps of Christ. These all hated their lives in this world, that they might keep them to life eternal.[3] How strict and self-denying was the life of the holy Fathers in the desert! How long and grievous the temptations they endured! How often they were assaulted by the Devil! How frequent and fervent their prayers to God! How strict their fasts! How great their zeal and ardour for spiritual progress! How valiant the battles they fought to overcome their vices! How pure and upright their intention towards God!

All day long they laboured, and the night they gave to continuous prayer; even as they worked, they never ceased from mental prayer. They spent all their time with profit, every hour seeming short in the service of God. They often forgot even their bodily needs in the great sweetness of contemplation. They renounced all riches, dignities, honours,

1. Wisd. iii, 6.   2. Heb. xi, 38; I Cor. iv, 11.   3. John xii, 25.

Although we cannot always preserve our recollection, yet we must do so from time to time, and at the least once a day, either in the morning or the evening. In the morning form your intention, and at night examine your conduct, what you have done, said, and thought during the day, for in each of these you may have often offended both God and your neighbour. Arm yourself manfully against the wickedness of the Devil;[1] control the appetite, and you will more easily control all bodily desires. Never be entirely idle, but be reading or writing, in prayer or in meditation, or else be engaged in some work for the common good. But undertake manual employments with discretion, for they are not to be practised by all men alike. Those spiritual exercises which are not obligatory should not be made in public; for whatever is purely personal is best done in private.

Take care not to become careless in the common observances, preferring your personal devotions. But when you have fully and faithfully fulfilled all that you are bound to do, then, if there be time left, employ it in your own devotions. All cannot use the same kind of spiritual exercises, but one suits this person, and another that. Different devotions are suited also to the Seasons, some being best for the Festivals, and others for ordinary days. We find some helpful in temptations, others in peace and quietness. Some things we like to consider when we are sad, and others when we are full of joy in the Lord.

At the great Festivals good spiritual exercises should be renewed, and the prayers of the Saints implored more fervently than ever. From one Festival to another we should resolve so to live, as though we were then to depart from this world and come to the heavenly Feast. During holy seasons, therefore, we should prepare ourselves with care, and live ever more devoutly, keeping every observance more strictly,

1. Eph. vi, 11.

as though we were soon to receive the reward of our labours from God Himself.

If this reward be delayed, let us consider that we are not yet ready or worthy of the great glory which will be revealed[1] in us at the appointed time : and let us strive to prepare ourselves better for our departure from this world, 'Blessed is the servant,' writes Luke the Evangelist, 'whom the Lord, when He comes, will find ready. I tell you truly that He will set him over all His possessions.'[2]

CHAPTER 20
On the Love of Solitude and Silence

CHOOSE a suitable time for recollection and frequently consider the loving-kindness of God. Do not read to satisfy curiosity or to pass the time, but study such things as move your heart to devotion. If you avoid unnecessary talk and aimless visits, listening to news and gossip, you will find plenty of suitable time to spend in meditation on holy things. The greatest Saints used to avoid the company of men[3] whenever they were able, and chose rather to serve God in solitude.

A wise man once said 'As often as I have been among men, I have returned home a lesser man.'[4] We often share this experience, when we spend much time in conversation. It is easier to keep silence altogether than not to talk more than we should. It is easier to remain quietly at home than to keep due watch over ourselves in public. Therefore, whoever is resolved to live an inward and spiritual life must, with Jesus, withdraw from the crowd.[5] No man can live in the public eye without risk to his soul, unless he who would prefer to remain obscure. No man can safely speak unless he who would

1. Rom. viii, 18.   4. Seneca, *Epist.* VII.
2. Matt. xxiv, 47.   5. Mark vi, 31.
3. Heb. xi, 38.

gladly remain silent. No man can safely command, unless he who has learned to obey well. No man can safely rejoice, unless he possesses the testimony of a good conscience.

The security of the Saints was grounded in the fear of God, nor were they less careful and humble because they were resplendent in great virtues and graces. But the security of the wicked springs from pride and presumption, and ends in self-deception. Never promise yourself security in this life, even though you seem to be a good monk or a devout hermit.

Those who stand highest in the esteem of men are most exposed to grievous peril, since they often have too great a confidence in themselves. It is therefore, more profitable to many that they should not altogether escape temptations, but be often assailed lest they become too secure and exalted in their pride, or turn too readily to worldly consolations. How good a conscience would he keep if a man never sought after passing pleasures nor became preoccupied with worldly affairs! If only a man could cast aside all useless anxiety and think only on divine and salutary things, how great would be his peace and tranquillity!

No one is worthy of heavenly comfort, unless they have diligently exercised themselves in holy contrition. If you desire heartfelt contrition, enter into your room, and shut out the clamour of the world, as it is written, 'Commune with your own heart, and in your chamber, and be still.'[1] Within your cell you will discover what you will only too often lose abroad. The cell that is dwelt in continually becomes a delight, but ill kept it breeds weariness of spirit. If in the beginning of your religious life you have dwelt in it and kept it well, it will later become a dear friend and a welcome comfort.

In silence and quietness the devout soul makes progress and learns the hidden mysteries of the Scriptures.[2] There she finds

1. Ps. iv, 4; Isa. xxvi, 20.   2. Ecclus. xxxix, 1-3.

floods of tears in which she may nightly wash and be cleansed.[1]
For the further she withdraws from all the tumult of the world,
the nearer she draws to her Maker. For God with His holy
angels will draw near to him who withdraws himself from his
friends and acquaintances. It is better to live in obscurity and
to seek the salvation of his soul, than to neglect this even to
work miracles. It is commendable in a Religious, therefore, to
go abroad but seldom, to avoid being seen, and to have no
desire to see men.

Why do you long to see that which is not lawful for you to
possess? The world itself passes away, and all the desires of it.[2]
The desires of the senses call you to roam abroad, but when
their hour is spent, what do you bring back but a burdened
conscience and a distracted heart? A cheerful going out often
brings a sad home-coming, and a merry evening brings a sorry
morning. For every bodily pleasure brings joy at first, but at
length it bites and destroys.[3]

What can you see elsewhere that you cannot see here?[4]
Look at the sky, the earth, and all the elements, for of these all
things are made. What can you see anywhere under the sun
that can endure for long? You hope, perhaps to find complete
satisfaction; but this you will never do. Were you to see all
things at present in existence spread out before your eyes, what
would it be but an unprofitable vision?[5] Lift up your eyes to
God on high,[6] and beg forgiveness for your sin and neglect-
fulness. Leave empty matters to the empty-headed, and give
your attention to those things that God commands you. Shut
your door upon you,[7] and call upon Jesus the Beloved.
Remain with Him in your cell, for you will not find so
great a peace anywhere else. Had you never gone out and
listened to idle talk, you would the better have remained

1. Ps. vi, 6.
2. 1 John ii, 17.
3. Prov. xxiii, 31, 32.
4. Eccles. i, 10.
5. Eccles. ii, 11.
6. Ps. cxxi, 1; Isa. xl, 26.
7. Matt. vi, 6;
Isa. xxvi, 20.

perfectly at peace. But if it pleases you to hear the news of the world, you must always suffer disquiet of heart as a result.

CHAPTER 21
On Contrition of Heart

IF you wish to grow in holiness, you must live in the fear of God.[1] Do not seek too much freedom, but discipline all your senses, and do not engage in foolish occupations; give yourself rather to contrition of heart, and you will find true devotion. Contrition reveals to us many good things to which dissipation rapidly blinds us. It is a wonder that any man can ever feel perfectly contented with this present life, if he weighs and considers his state of banishment, and the many perils which beset his soul.

Levity of heart and neglect of our faults make us insensible to the proper sorrows of the soul, and we often engage in empty laughter when we should rightly weep. There is no real liberty and true joy, save in the fear of God with a quiet conscience. Happy is he who can set aside every hindering distraction, and recall himself to the single purpose of contrition. Happy is he who abjures whatever may stain or burden his conscience. Fight manfully, for one habit overcomes another. If you are content to let others alone, they will gladly leave you to accomplish your purpose unhindered.

Do not busy yourself with the affairs of others, nor concern yourself with the policies of your superiors. Watch yourself at all times, and correct yourself before you correct your friends.

Do not be grieved if you do not enjoy popular favour; grieve rather that you do not live as well and carefully as befits a servant of God, and a devout religious person. It is often

1. Prov. i, 7; xix, 23.

53

better and safer not to have many comforts in this life, especially those of the body. Yet, if we seldom or never feel God's comfort, the fault is our own; for we neither seek contrition of heart, nor entirely forego all vain and outward consolations.

Consider yourself unworthy of God's comfort, but rather deserving of much suffering. When a man is perfectly contrite, this present world becomes grievous and bitter to him. A good man always finds cause for grief and tears; for whether he considers himself or his neighbours, he knows that no man lives without trouble in this life. And the more strictly he examines himself, the more cause he finds for sorrow. Our sins and vices are grounds for rightful sorrow and contrition of heart; for they have so strong a hold on us that we are seldom able to contemplate heavenly things.

If you had more concern for a holy death than a long life, you would certainly be zealous to live better. And were you to ponder in your mind on the pains of Hell and Purgatory,[1] you would readily endure toil and sorrow, and would shrink from no kind of hardship. But because considerations of this kind do not move the heart, we remain cold and unresponsive, clinging to old delights.

It is often our lack of spiritual life that allows our wretched body to rebel so easily. Humbly beg Our Lord, therefore, to grant you the spirit of contrition, and say with the Prophet, 'Feed me, O Lord, with the bread of tears, and give me plenteousness of tears to drink.'[2]

1. Matt. xxv, 41.   2. Ps. lxxx, 5.

CHAPTER 22

On Human Misery

WHEREVER you are and wherever you turn, you will not find happiness until you turn to God. Why are you so distressed when events do not turn out as you wish and hope? Is there anyone who enjoys everything as he wishes? Neither you, nor I, nor anyone else on earth. There is no one in the world without trouble or anxiety, be he King or Pope. Whose, then, is the happiest lot? Surely, he who is able to suffer for love of God.

Many weak and foolish people[1] say, 'See what a good life that man enjoys! He is so rich, so great, so powerful, so distinguished!' But raise your eyes to the riches of Heaven, and you will see that all the riches of this world are as nothing. All are uncertain and even burdensome, for they are never enjoyed without some anxiety or fear. The happiness of man does not consist in abundance of this world's goods,[2] for a modest share is sufficient for him. The more spiritual a man desires to become, the more bitter does this present life grow for him, for he sees and realizes more clearly the defects and corruptions of human nature. For to eat and drink, to wake and sleep, to rest and labour, and to be subject to all the necessities of nature is a great trouble and affliction to the devout man, who would rather be released and set free from all sin.[3]

The inner life of man is greatly hindered in this life by the needs of the body. Thus, the Prophet devoutly prays that he may be set free from them, saying, 'Lord, deliver me from my necessities!'[4] Woe to those who refuse to recognize their own wretchedness, and doubly woe to those who love this miserable and corruptible life![5] For some cling so closely to it,

1. Luke xii, 19.
2. Prov. xix, 1.
3. Rom. vii, 24; 2 Cor. v, 2.
4. Ps. xxv, 16.
5. Rom. viii, 21.

that although by working or begging they can hardly win the bare necessities, they would yet be willing to live here for ever if it were possible, caring nothing for the Kingdom of God.

How crazy and lacking in faith are such people, who are so deeply engrossed in earthly affairs that they care for nothing but material things![1] These unhappy wretches will at length know to their sorrow how vile and worthless were the things that they loved. But the Saints of God and all the devoted friends of Christ paid little heed to bodily pleasures, nor to prosperity in this life, for all their hopes and aims were directed towards those good things that are eternal.[2] Their whole desire raised them upward to things eternal and invisible, so that the love of things visible could not drag them down. My brother, do not lose hope of progress in the spiritual life;[3] you have still time and opportunity.

Why put off your good resolution? Rise and begin this very moment, and say, 'Now is the time to be up and doing; now is the time to fight; now is the time to amend.'[4] When things go badly and you are in trouble, then is the time to win merit. You must pass through fire and water, before you can come into the place of rest.[5] You will never overcome your vices, unless you discipline yourself severely. For so long as we wear this frail body, we cannot be without sin, nor can we live without weariness and sorrow. We would gladly be free from all troubles; but since we have lost our innocence through sin, we have also lost true happiness. We must therefore have patience,[6] and wait for God's mercy, until this wickedness pass away, and death be swallowed up in life.[7]

How great is the frailty of man, ever prone to evil![8] Today you confess your sins; tomorrow you again commit the very

1. Rom. viii, 5. 4. 2 Cor. vi, 2. 7. 2 Cor. v, 4.
2. 1 Pet. i, 4. 5. Ps. lxvi, 11. 8. Gen. vi, 5.
3. Heb. x, 35. 6. Heb. x, 36.

sins you have confessed! Now you resolve to guard against them, and within the hour you act as though you had never made any resolution! Remembering, then, our weakness and instability, it is proper to humble ourselves, and never to have a high opinion of ourselves. For we can easily lose by carelessness that which by God's grace and our own efforts we had hardly won.

What will become of us in the end if our zeal so quickly grows cold? Unhappy our fate, if we rest on our oars as though we had already reached a haven of peace and security,[1] when in fact no sign of holiness is apparent in our lives. It would be good for us to be instructed once more, like good novices, in the ways of the good life; there would then be some hope of our future improvement and greater spiritual progress.

CHAPTER 23
A Meditation on Death

VERY soon the end of your life will be at hand: consider, therefore, the state of your soul. Today a man is here; tomorrow he is gone.[2] And when he is out of sight, he is soon out of mind. Oh, how dull and hard is the heart of man, which thinks only of the present, and does not provide against the future! You should order your every deed and thought, as though today were the day of your death. Had you a good conscience, death would hold no terrors for you;[3] even so, it were better to avoid sin than to escape death.[4] If you are not ready to die today, will tomorrow find you better prepared?[5] Tomorrow is uncertain; and how can you be sure of tomorrow?

1. I Thess. v, 3.   3. Luke xii, 37.   5. Matt. xxiv, 44.
2. I Macc. ii, 63.   4. Wisd. iv, 16.

Of what use is a long life, if we amend so little? Alas, a long life often adds to our sins rather than to our virtue!

Would to God that we might spend a single day really well! Many recount the years since their conversion, but their lives show little sign of improvement. If it is dreadful to die, it is perhaps more dangerous to live long. Blessed is the man who keeps the hour of his death always in mind, and daily prepares himself to die. If you have ever seen anyone die, remember that you, too, must travel the same road.[1]

Each morning remember that you may not live until evening; and in the evening, do not presume to promise yourself another day. Be ready at all times,[2] and so live that death may never find you unprepared. Many die suddenly and unexpectedly; for at an hour that we do not know the Son of Man will come.[3] When your last hour strikes, you will begin to think very differently of your past life, and grieve deeply that you have been so careless and remiss.

Happy and wise is he who endeavours to be during his life as he wishes to be found at his death. For these things will afford us sure hope of a happy death; perfect contempt of the world; fervent desire to grow in holiness; love of discipline; the practice of penance; ready obedience; self-denial; the bearing of every trial for the love of Christ. While you enjoy health, you can do much good; but when sickness comes, little can be done. Few are made better by sickness, and those who make frequent pilgrimages seldom acquire holiness by so doing.

Do not rely on friends and neighbours, and do not delay the salvation of your soul to some future date, for men will forget you sooner than you think. It is better to make timely provision and to acquire merit in this life, than to depend on the help of others. And if you have no care for your own soul, who will have care for you in time to come? The present time

1. Heb. ix, 27.　　　2. Luke xxi, 36.　　　3. Matt. xxiv, 44.

is most precious; now is the accepted time, now is the day of salvation.[1] It is sad that you do not employ your time better, when you may win eternal life hereafter. The time will come when you will long for one day or one hour in which to amend; and who knows whether it will be granted?

Dear soul, from what peril and fear you could free yourself, if you lived in holy fear, mindful of your death. Apply yourself so to live now, that at the hour of death, you may be glad and unafraid. Learn now to die to the world, that you may begin to live with Christ.[2] Learn now to despise all earthly things, that you may go freely to Christ. Discipline your body now by penance, that you may enjoy a sure hope of salvation.

Foolish man, how can you promise yourself a long life, when you are not certain of a single day?[3] How many have deceived themselves in this way, and been snatched unexpectedly from life! You have often heard how this man was slain by the sword; another drowned; how another fell from a high place and broke his neck; how another died at table; how another met his end in play. One perishes by fire, another by the sword, another from disease, another at the hands of robbers. Death is the end of all men;[4] and the life of man passes away suddenly as a shadow.[5]

Who will remember you when you are dead? Who will pray for you? Act now, dear soul; do all you can; for you know neither the hour of your death, nor your state after death. While you have time, gather the riches of everlasting life.[6] Think only of your salvation, and care only for the things of God. Make friends now, by honouring the Saints of God and by following their example, that when this life is over, they may welcome you to your eternal home.[7]

1. 2 Cor. vi, 2.
2. Rom. vi, 8.
3. Luke xii, 20.
4. Eccles. vii. 2.
5. Ps. xxxix, 7; cxliv, 4.
6. Luke xii, 33; Gal. vi, 8.
7. Luke xvi, 9.

Keep yourself a stranger and pilgrim upon earth,[1] to whom the affairs of this world are of no concern. Keep your heart free and lifted up to God, for here you have no abiding city.[2] Daily direct your prayers and longings to Heaven, that at your death your soul may merit to pass joyfully into the presence of God.

CHAPTER 24
On Judgement, and the Punishment of Sinners

ALWAYS keep in mind your last end, and how you will stand before the just Judge[3] from whom nothing is hid, who cannot be influenced by bribes and excuses, and who judges with justice.[4] O wretched and foolish sinner, who tremble before the anger of man, how will you answer to God,[5] who knows all your wickedness? Why do you not prepare yourself against the Day of Judgement, when no advocate can defend or excuse you, but each man will be hard put to answer for himself? While you live, your labour is profitable and your tears acceptable, for sorrow both cleanses the soul and makes peace with God.

The patient man undergoes a great and wholesome purgation; while suffering injuries, he grieves yet more for the malice of others than for his own wrongs; he gladly prays for his enemies, and from his heart forgives their offences; he does not hesitate to ask pardon of others; he is more easily moved to compassion than to anger; he rules himself with strictness, and endeavours to make the body subject to the spirit in all things. It is better to expiate our sins and overcome our vices now, than to reserve them for purgation hereafter; but we deceive ourselves by our inordinate love of the body.

1. 1 Pet. ii, 11. 3. Heb. x, 31. 5. Job xxxi, 14.
2. Heb. xiii, 14. 4. Isa. xi, 4.

What will the flames feed upon, but your sins? The more you spare yourself now, and indulge the desires of the body, the more severe will be your punishment hereafter, and the more fuel you gather for the flames. In whatever things a man sins, in those will he be the more severely punished.[1] Then will the slothful be spurred by fiery goads, and the gluttonous tormented by dire hunger and thirst. Then will the luxurious and pleasure-loving be plunged into burning pitch and stinking sulphur, while the envious will howl their grief like wild dogs.

There is no vice that will not receive its proper retribution. The proud will be subjected to the deepest humiliation, and the greedy experience misery and want. One hour's punishment then will be more bitter than a century of penance on earth. There will be neither rest nor comfort for the damned; but here we sometimes enjoy rest from our toil, and enjoy the comfort of our friends. Therefore, live rightly now, and grieve for your sins, that in the Day of Judgement you may stand secure in the company of the Blessed. For then shall the righteous stand with great boldness before those who have afflicted and oppressed them.[2] Then will he who now submits humbly to the judgement of man stand to judge others. Then will the poor and humble have great confidence, while the proud are encompassed by fears on every side.

It will then be seen that he who learned to be counted a fool and despised for Christ's sake in this world was indeed wise.[3] Then will he be glad for every trial patiently borne, and the mouth of the wicked will be sealed.[4] Then will every devout man be glad and the ungodly grieve. Then will he who kept his body in subjection[5] have greater joy than he who lavished every pleasure upon it. Then will the rags of the poor shine with splendour, and the gorgeous raiment become tarnished.

1. Wisd. xi, 17.   3. 1 Cor. iv, 10.   5. 1 Cor. ix, 27.
2. Wisd. v, 1.   4. Ps. cvii, 42.

Then will the humble cottage of the poor be preferred to the gilded palace. Then will steadfast patience be of more avail than all worldly power. Then will humble obedience be exalted above all wordly cunning. Then will a good and clean conscience bring more joy than learned philosophy. Then will contempt for riches far outweigh all the treasures of the world. Then will devout prayer yield greater pleasure than fine fare. Then will you rejoice more in having kept silence than in much talking. Then will holy deeds count for more than fine words. Then will a disciplined life and hard penance prove of more worth than all worldly delights.

Learn to endure a little now, that you may spare yourself more grievous troubles. Prove here what you can endure hereafter. If you can endure so little now, how could you endure the pains of hell? Be assured that a man cannot enjoy both kinds of happiness; he cannot enjoy all the pleasures of this life, and also reign with Christ in Heaven. Moreover, if up to this very day you had lived in enjoyment of all honours and pleasures, how would all these profit you if you were to die at this moment? All, therefore, is vanity, save to love God and serve Him alone. For he who loves God with all his heart fears neither death, punishment, judgement, nor hell; for perfect love enjoys sure access to God.[1] But he who continues to delight in wickedness, what wonder is it if he fears death and judgement? Nevertheless, it is good that, if the love of God does not restrain you from sin, the fear of hell at least should restrain you. For he who sets aside the fear of God cannot long continue in a good life, but will rapidly fall into the snares of the Devil.

1. Rom. viii, 39.

CHAPTER 25

On the Zealous Amendment of our Life

BE watchful[1] and diligent in the service of God, and frequently consider why you are come here, and why you have renounced the world. Was it not that you might live to God, and become a spiritual man? Endeavour, then, to make progress, and you will soon receive the reward of your labours; then neither fear nor sorrow will be able to trouble you. Labour for a short while now, and you will find great peace of soul, and everlasting joy. If you remain faithful in all your doings, be sure that God will be faithful and generous in rewarding you.[2] Keep a firm hope that you will win the victor's crown; but do not be over confident, lest you become indolent and self-satisfied.

There was once a man who was very anxious, and wavered between fear and hope. One day, overcome with sadness, he lay prostrate in prayer before the altar in church, and pondering these matters in his mind, said, 'Oh, if only I knew that I should always persevere!' then he heard within his heart an answer from God: 'If you knew this, what would you do? Do now what you would then, and all will be well.' So, comforted and strengthened, he committed himself to the will of God, and his anxious uncertainty vanished. Nor did he wish any longer to inquire into what would happen to him, but strove the more earnestly to learn the perfect and acceptable will of God,[3] whenever he began or undertook any good work.[4]

'Hope in the Lord, and do good,' says the Prophet: 'dwell in the land, and you shall be fed with its riches.'[5] There is one thing that deters many in their spiritual progress and zeal for amendment, namely, fear of the difficulties and the cost of victory. But rest assured that those who grow in virtue beyond

1. 2 Tim. iv, 5.   3. Rom. xii, 2.   5. Ps. xxxvii, 3.
2. Ecclus li, 30.   4. 2 Tim. iii, 17.

their fellows are they who fight most manfully to overcome whatever is most difficult and distasteful to them. For the more completely a man overcomes and cleanses himself in spirit, the more he profits and deserves abundant grace.

All men do not have the same things to overcome and mortify. But whoever is diligent and zealous – even though he has stronger passions to subdue – will certainly make greater progress than another, who is naturally self-controlled, but less zealous for holiness. Two things in particular are a great help to amendment of life – a forcible withdrawal from any vice to which our nature inclines, and a fervent pursuit of any grace of which we stand in particular need. Especially study to avoid and overcome those things that most displease you in other people.

Strive to progress in all things, and let any examples that you see or hear inspire you to imitate them. But if you observe anything blameworthy, take care not to do the same yourself. And should you ever have done so, amend your conduct without delay. As you observe others, so do others observe you.[1] How glad and pleasant it is to see fervent and devout brethren observing good manners and good discipline.[2] And how sad and painful to see any who are disorderly and fail to live up to their calling. How harmful it is, if they neglect the true purpose of their vocation, and turn to matters that are not their proper concern.

Remember your avowed purpose, and keep ever before you the likeness of Christ crucified. As you meditate on the life of Jesus Christ, you should grieve that you have not tried more earnestly to conform yourself to Him, although you have been a long while in the way of God. A Religious who earnestly and devoutly contemplates the most holy Life and Passion of Our Lord will find it in an abundance of all things profitable and needful to him, nor need he seek any other model than

1. Matt. vii, 3.   2. Eph. v, 2.

Jesus. Oh, if Jesus Crucified would come into our hearts, how quickly and fully we should be instructed!

A zealous Religious readily accepts and obeys all commands. But a careless and lukewarm Religious has trouble after trouble, and finds sorrow on every side because he lacks true inward consolation, and is forbidden to seek it outside. Therefore a Religious who disregards his Rule exposes himself to dreadful ruin. And he who desires an easier and undisciplined life will always be unstable, for one thing or another will always displease him.

Observe how many behave, who live strictly under the monastic discipline. They seldom go out, they live retired, they eat the poorest food; they work hard, they talk little, they keep long watches; they rise early, they spend much time in prayer, they study much, and always guard themselves with discipline. Consider the Carthusians, the Cistercians, and the monks and nuns of the various Orders, how they rise each night to sing praises to Our Lord. Were you slothful, this should shame you, when so great a company of Religious are beginning the praises of God.

Would that our sole occupation were the perpetual praise of the Lord our God with heart and voice! Had you no need of food, drink or rest, you could praise God without ceasing, and give yourself wholly to spiritual things. You would be far happier than now, when you are compelled to serve the needs of the body. Would that these needs did not exist, so that we might enjoy the spiritual feasts of the soul, which, alas, we taste so seldom.

When a man no longer seeks his comfort from any creature, then he first begins to enjoy God perfectly, and he will be well content with whatever befalls him. Then he will neither rejoice over having much, nor grieve over having little, but will commit himself fully and trustfully to God, who is All[1] in all

1. Col. iii, 11.

to him: in Him nothing perishes or dies, for all things live for Him, and serve His will continually.

Always remember your end,[1] and that lost time never returns. Without care and diligence, you will never acquire virtue. If you begin to grow careless, all will begin to go amiss with you. But if you give yourself to prayer, you will find great peace, and your toil will grow lighter by the help of God's grace and your love of virtue. The fervent and sincere man is prepared for anything. The war against our vices and passions is harder than any physical toil; and whoever fails to overcome his lesser faults will gradually fall into greater.[2] Your evenings will always be tranquil if you have spent the day well. Watch yourself, bestir yourself, admonish yourself; and whatever others may do, never neglect your own soul. The stricter you are with yourself, the greater is your spiritual progress.

1. Ecclus. vii, 36.   2. Ecclus. xix, 1.

BOOK TWO

COUNSELS ON THE
INNER LIFE

CHAPTER I
On the Inner Life

'THE Kingdom of God is within you,'[1] says Our Lord. Turn
to the Lord with all your heart,[2] forsake this sorry world, and
your soul shall find rest.[3] Learn to turn from worldly things,
and give yourself to spiritual things, and you will see the Kingdom of God come within you. For the Kingdom is peace and
joy in the Holy Spirit;[4] these are not granted to the wicked.
Christ will come to you, and impart his consolations to you, if
you prepare a worthy dwelling for Him in your heart. All
true glory and beauty is within,[5] and there He delights to
dwell. He often visits the spiritual man, and holds sweet discourse with him, granting him refreshing grace, great peace,
and friendship exceeding all expectation.

Come then, faithful soul; prepare your heart for your
Divine Spouse, that He may deign to come to you and dwell
with you. For He says, 'If any man love Me, he will keep My
word; and We will come and make Our abode with him.'[6]
Therefore welcome Christ, and deny entrance to all others.
When you possess Christ, you are amply rich, and He will
satisfy you. He will dispose and provide for you faithfully in
everything, so that you need not rely on man. For men soon

1. Luke xvii, 21.   3. Matt. xi, 29.   5. Ps. xlv, 14.
2. Joel ii, 12.   4. Rom. xiv, 17.   6. John xiv, 23.

change and fail you; but Christ abides for ever,[1] and stands firmly by you to the end.

Never place your whole trust and reliance in weak and mortal man, however helpful and dear to you he may be; nor should you grieve overmuch if sometimes he opposes and contradicts you. Those who take your part today may tomorrow oppose you; for men are as changeable as the weather. Put your whole trust in God;[2] direct your worship and love to Him alone. He will defend you, and will dispose all things for the best. Here you have no abiding city,[3] and wherever you may be, you are a stranger and pilgrim;[4] you will never enjoy peace until you become inwardly united to Christ.

What do you seek here, since this world is not your resting place? Your true home is in Heaven;[5] therefore remember that all the things of this world are transitory. All things are passing, and yourself with them. See that you do not cling to them, lest you become entangled and perish with them. Let all your thoughts be with the Most High, and direct your humble prayers unceasingly to Christ. If you cannot contemplate high and heavenly things, take refuge in the Passion of Christ, and love to dwell within His Sacred Wounds. For if you devoutly seek the Wounds of Jesus and the precious marks of His Passion, you will find great strength in all troubles. And if men despise you, you will care little, having small regard for the words of your detractors.

Christ Himself was despised by men, and in His direst need was abandoned by his friends and acquaintances to the insults of His enemies. Christ was willing to suffer and to be despised; and do you presume to complain? Christ had enemies and slanderers; and do you expect all men to be your friends and benefactors? How will your patience be crowned, if you are

1. John xii, 34.   3. Heb. xiii, 14.   5. Phil. iii, 20.
2. Prov. iii, 5; 1 Pet.   4. Heb. xi, 13.
   v, 7.

not willing to endure hardship? Suffer with Christ, and for Christ, if you wish to reign with Christ.[1]

Had you but once entered perfectly into the Heart of Jesus, and tasted something of His burning love, you would care nothing for your own gain or loss; for the love of Jesus causes a man to regard himself very humbly. The true, inward lover of Jesus and the Truth, who is free from inordinate desires, can turn freely to God, rise above self, and joyfully rest in God.

He who knows all things at their true worth, and not as they are said or reputed to be, is truly wise,[2] for his knowledge comes from God, and not from man. He who walks by an inner light, and is not unduly influenced by outward things, needs no special time or place for his prayers. For the man of inner life easily recollects himself, since he is never wholly immersed in outward affairs. Therefore his outward occupations and needful tasks do not distract him, and he adjusts himself to things as they come. The man whose inner life is well-ordered and disposed is not troubled by the strange and perverse ways of others; for a man is hindered and distracted by such things only so far as he allows himself to be concerned by them.

If your inner life were rightly ordered and your heart pure, all things would turn to your good and advantage.[3] As it is, you are often displeased and disturbed, because you are not yet completely dead to self, nor detached from all worldly things. Nothing defiles and ensnares the heart of man more than a selfish love of creatures. If you renounce all outward consolation, you will be able to contemplate heavenly things, and often experience great joy of heart.

1. 2 Tim. ii, 12.   2. Isa. liv, 13.   3. Rom. viii, 28.

CHAPTER 2

On Humble Submission to God

Do not be concerned overmuch who is with you or against you, but work and plan that God may be with you in all that you do.[1] Keep a clean conscience, and God will mightily defend you; for whoever enjoys the protection of God cannot be harmed by the malice of man. If you learn to suffer in silence, you may be sure of receiving God's help.[2] He knows the time and the way to deliver you; so trust yourself entirely to His care. God is strong to help you, and to free you from all confusion. It is often good for us that others know and expose our faults, for so may we be kept humble.

When a man humbly admits his faults, he soon appeases his fellows, and is reconciled to those whom he had offended. God protects and delivers a humble man; He loves and comforts him.[3] To the humble He leans down and bestows great success, raising him from abasement to honour. To him He reveals His secrets,[4] and lovingly calls and draws him to Himself. Even in the midst of trouble, the humble man remains wholly at peace, for he trusts in God, and not in the world. Do not consider yourself to have made any spiritual progress, unless you account yourself the least of all men.

CHAPTER 3

On the Good and Peaceful Man

FIRSTLY, be peaceful yourself, and you will be able to bring peace to others. A man of peace does more good than a very learned man. A passionate man turns even good into evil, and readily listens to evil; but a good and peaceable man

1. Rom. viii, 31.   3. 1 Pet. v, 5; James   4. Matt. xi, 25.
2. 2 Cor. vii, 6.   iv, 6.

turns all things to good. He who is truly at peace thinks evil of no one; but he who is discontented and restless is tormented by suspicions beyond number. He has no peace in himself, nor will he allow others any peace. He often says what he ought not to say, and leaves undone what he should have done. He takes note how other people carry out their duties, but neglects his own. Therefore, before all else, attend diligently to your own affairs; then you may properly be concerned for your neighbour also.

You readily excuse and explain your own doings, but you will not accept the explanations of others. It would be more just to accuse yourself, and to excuse your fellows. If you wish others to bear with you, you must bear with them.[1] See how far you still are from true charity and humility, which feels no anger nor indignation towards any save itself. It is no great matter to associate with the good and gentle, for this is naturally pleasant to everyone. All men are glad to live at peace, and prefer those who are of their own way of thinking. But to be able to live at peace among hard, obstinate, and un-disciplined people and those who oppose us, is a great grace, and a most commendable and manly achievement.

There are some who remain at peace with themselves and also with others.[2] And some neither have peace in themselves nor allow others to have peace. Such people are a trouble to others, and an even greater trouble to themselves. And there are some who are at peace with themselves, and who try to guide others into peace. But all our peace in this present life should depend on humble forbearance rather than on absence of adversity. He who knows the secret of endurance will enjoy the greatest peace. Such a one is conqueror of self, master of the world, a friend of Christ, and an heir of Heaven.

1. Gal. vi, 2; 1 Cor.   2. Rom. xii, 18; 2
   xiii, 7; Eph. iv, 2.   Cor. xiii, 11.

CHAPTER 4
On Purity of Mind and Simplicity of Purpose

THERE are two wings that raise a man above earthly things – simplicity and purity. Simplicity must inspire his purpose, and purity his affection. Simplicity reaches out after God; purity discovers and enjoys Him. No good deed will prove an obstacle to you if you are inwardly free from uncontrolled desires. And if you are free from uncontrolled desires, and seek nothing but the Will of God and the good of your neighbour, you will enjoy this inner freedom. If your heart be right, then every created thing will become for you a mirror of life and a book of holy teaching. For there is nothing created so small and mean that it does not reflect the goodness of God.

Were you inwardly good and pure, you would see and understand all things clearly and without difficulty. A pure heart penetrates both heaven and hell. As each man is in himself, so does he judge outward things. If there is any joy to be had in this world, the pure in heart most surely possess it; and if there is trouble and distress anywhere,[1] the evil conscience most readily experiences it. Just as iron, when plunged into fire, loses its rust and becomes bright and glowing, so the man who turns himself wholly to God loses his sloth and becomes transformed into a new creature.

When a man begins to grow dull and lukewarm in spirit, even the smallest labour distresses him, and he eagerly welcomes any worldly comfort. But when he begins to overcome self and advance manfully in God's way, then he regards as nothing those labours which he previously found so burdensome.

1. Rom. ii, 9.

CHAPTER 5
On Knowing Ourselves

WE may not trust overmuch in ourselves, for we often lack grace and understanding. There is little light in us, and even this we easily lose through carelessness. Moreover, we often do not realize how blind we are. We often do evil, and we do worse in excusing ourselves. Sometimes we are moved by passion, and mistake it for Zeal. We rebuke small faults in others, but overlook greater faults in ourselves.[1] We are too quick to resent and feel what we suffer from others, but fail to consider how much others suffer from us. Whoever considers his own defects fully and honestly will find no reason to judge others harshly.

The spiritual man puts the care of his soul before all else;[2] and whoever diligently attends to his own affairs is ready to keep silence about others. You will never become interior and devout unless you refrain from criticism of others, and pay attention to yourself. If you are wholly intent on God and yourself, you will be little affected by anything outside this.[3] Where are you when you fail to attend to yourself? And when you have occupied yourself in countless affairs, what have you gained, if you have neglected your soul?[4] If you really desire true peace and union with God, attend to yourself, and set aside all else.

Keep yourself free from all worldly entanglement, and you will make good progress; but if you set great value on any wordly things, it will prove a great obstacle. Let nothing be great, pleasant or desirable to you save God alone, and whatever comes of God. Regard as empty comfort all things that derive from creatures. The soul that loves God regards as worthless all things other than God. God alone is eternal and

1. Matt. vii, 5. 3. 1 Cor. iv, 3.
2. Matt. xvi, 26. 4. Mark viii, 36.

73

immeasurable, filling all things;¹ He alone is the true comfort of the soul and joy of the heart.

CHAPTER 6

On the Joys of a Good Conscience

THE glory of a good man is the witness of a good conscience.² Preserve a quiet conscience, and you will always have joy. A quiet conscience can endure much, and remains joyful in all trouble, but an evil conscience is always fearful and uneasy.³ You may rest easy if your heart does not reproach you, and you are happy only when you have done right. The wicked never know true happiness, nor do they enjoy inward peace, for 'There is no peace for the wicked,'⁴ says the Lord. And although they say, 'We are at peace; no evil happens to us, and no one will dare to harm us,' yet God's anger will rise suddenly, all their works will be brought to nothing, and their plans perish.

To glory in suffering is not hard for one who truly loves God, for so to glory is to glory in the Cross of our Lord.⁵ Short-lived is the glory that is granted and received by men, and sorrow is ever its companion. The glory of good men is in their own conscience, not in the tongues of men. For the joy of the Saints is from God and in God, and their joy is in the truth.⁶ Whoever desires true and lasting glory cares nothing for worldly glory. And whoever craves worldly glory, or who does not at heart despise it, shows himself to have little love for the glory of heaven. Great tranquillity of heart is his who cares for neither praise nor blame.

The man who has a clean conscience rests easily content,

1. Jer. xxiii, 24.   4. Isa. xlviii, 22.   6. 1 Cor. xiii, 6.
2. 2 Cor. i, 12.   5. Rom. v, 3; Gal. v,
3. 1 John iii, 21.   14.

and is at peace. You are none the holier for being praised, and none the worse for being blamed. You remain what you are, nor can you be accounted greater than you are in the sight of God. If you take heed to what you are inwardly, you will not mind what men say of you; for while man looks on outward appearance, God looks into your heart. Man sees your actions, but God your motives. The sign of a humble soul is always to be doing good, and to think little of oneself. To desire no comfort from creatures is a sign of great purity and inward faith.

When a man seeks no other witness but himself, he shows that he puts his whole trust in God. For, as Saint Paul says, 'Not he who commends himself is approved, but he whom God commends.'[1] To live inwardly to God, and not to be bound by worldly affections, is the proper state of a spiritual man.

CHAPTER 7

On Loving Jesus above all Things

BLESSED is he who understands what it is to love Jesus, and to despise himself for Jesus' sake. You must surrender all other love for His love, for Jesus desires to be loved alone, and above all things. The love of creatures is deceptive and unstable; the love of Jesus is faithful and enduring. Whoever clings to any creature will fall with its falling; but he who holds to Jesus shall stand firm for ever. Love Him, therefore, and keep Him as your friend; for when all others desert you, He will not abandon you, nor allow you to perish at the last. Whether you wish it or not, you must in the end be parted from them all.

Hold fast to Jesus, both in life and death, and trust yourself to His faithfulness, for He alone can aid you when all others

1. 2 Cor. x, 18.

fail. Your Beloved is of such a nature that He will not share your love with another; He desires your heart for Himself alone, and to reign there as a King on His throne. If you could empty your heart of all creatures, Jesus would delight to dwell with you.[1] Whatever trust you place in men rather than in Jesus is almost wholly wasted. Do not trust or lean on a windblown reed,[2] for 'all flesh is as grass, and its glory will fall like the flower of the grass.'[3]

If you look only to men's outward appearance, you will soon be deceived; for if you seek comfort or gain from others, you will often meet with loss. If you seek Jesus in all things, you will surely find Jesus. And if you seek yourself, you will surely find yourself, but only to your ruin. For a man who does not seek Jesus does himself greater hurt than the whole world and all his enemies could ever do him.

CHAPTER 8

On Close Friendship with Jesus

WHEN Jesus is with us, all is well, and nothing seems hard; but when Jesus is absent, everything is difficult. When Jesus does not speak to the heart, all other comfort is unavailing; but if Jesus speaks but a single word, we are greatly comforted. Did not Mary Magdalene rise at once from the place where she wept, when Martha said, 'The Master is come, and is asking for you'?[4] Oh, happy the hour when Jesus calls us from tears to joy of spirit! How arid and hard of heart you are without Jesus! How foolish and empty if you desire anything but Jesus! Surely, this is a greater injury to you than the loss of the whole world!

1. John xv, 4.
2. Isa. xxxvi, 6; Matt.
   xi, 7; Luke vii, 24.
3. Isa. xl, 6; Ecclus.
   xiv, 18; James i, 10;
   1 Pet. i, 24.
4. John xi, 28.

What can the world offer you, without Jesus? To be without Jesus is hell most grievous; to be with Jesus is to know the sweetness of Heaven. If Jesus is with you, no enemy can harm you. Whoever finds Jesus, finds a rich treasure, and a good above every good. He who loses Jesus, loses much indeed, and more than the whole world. Poorest of all men is he who lives without Jesus, and richest of all is he who stands in favour with Jesus.

It is a great art to know how to hold converse with Jesus, and to know how to keep Jesus is wisdom indeed. Be humble and a man of peace, and Jesus will abide with you. But if you turn aside to worldly things, you will soon cause Jesus to leave you, and you will lose His grace. And if you drive Him away and lose Him, with whom may you take refuge, and whom will you seek for your friend? Without a friend, you cannot live happily, and if Jesus is not your best friend, you will be exceedingly sad and lonely; so it is foolish to trust or delight in any other. It is better to have the whole world as your enemy, than offend Jesus. Therefore, of all dear friends, let Jesus be loved first and above all.

Love all men for Jesus' sake, but Jesus for Himself. Jesus Christ alone is to be loved with an especial love, for He alone is the best and most faithful of friends. In Him and for His sake love both friend and foe, and pray to Him for all of them, that all may know and love Him. Do not wish to become the object of especial praise or love, for this belongs to God alone, who has none like Himself. Do not desire that the heart of anyone be given wholly to yourself, and do not yield yourself wholly to the love of anyone; rather, let Jesus abide in you, and in every good person.

Be pure and free of heart, untrammelled by any created thing. Offer to God a pure and spotless heart, if you wish to be at liberty, and see how gracious the Lord is. Unless His grace draw and guide you, you will never attain this; but once you

have cast aside and forsaken all else, you may be united to
Him alone. When the grace of God comes to a man, he is
strong in all things; but when it departs, he is left poor and
weak, and feels abandoned to punishment and sorrow. When
this happens to you, do not despair or be discouraged, but
accept God's will calmly, bearing all that befalls you for the
glory of Christ; for after winter comes summer, night turns to
day, and after a storm comes fair weather.[1]

CHAPTER 9

On the Lack of all Comfort

IT is not difficult to forego human comfort when we enjoy
that of God. But it is a great thing to be able to forego all
consolation, human or divine, and for God's sake willingly to
endure desolation of heart, neither seeking oneself in anything,
nor regarding one's own merit. Is it any proof of virtue that
you are filled with joy and devotion when God sends His
grace? Surely, everyone longs for this; for he rides at ease
who is borne up by the grace of God. Is it any wonder that he
feels no weariness, when he is carried by the Almighty, and
led by the greatest of all Leaders?[2]

We are always glad of comfort, and only with difficulty is a
man stripped of self-love. The holy martyr Laurence, with his
priest, overcame the world, because he despised all that seemed
delightful in the world. For the love of Christ, he patiently
allowed God's high-priest Sixtus, whom he dearly loved, to be
taken from him. Thus, by love of the Creator, he conquered
his love for man, and preferred the will of God to all the
comforts of men. So also must you learn to give up even your
close and beloved friend for the love of God. And do not

1. Ps. cvii, 29; Matt. viii, 26.   2. Deut. i, 30.

grieve when a friend deserts you, for we must all be parted from one another at last.

A man has to undergo a long and fierce inner struggle before he learns fully to master himself, and to direct his whole love towards God. When a man relies on himself, he often comes to rely on human consolations. But the true lover of Christ and the eager seeker after holiness does not fall back on these things, nor does he look for pleasurable sensations, but prefers to endure great trials and arduous toil for Christ.

When God bestows spiritual comfort, receive it with a grateful heart; but remember that it comes of God's free gift, and not of your own merit. Do not be proud, nor over joyful, nor foolishly presumptuous; rather, be the more humble for this gift, more cautious, and more prudent in all your doings, for this hour will pass, and temptation will follow it. When comfort is withdrawn, do not immediately despair, but humbly and patiently await the will of Heaven; for God is able to restore to you a consolation even richer than before. This is nothing new or strange to those who know the ways of God, for the great Saints and Prophets of old often experienced these changes.

When grace was with him, David once exclaimed, 'In my prosperity I said, I shall never be removed.'[1] But when grace was withdrawn, he tells what he experienced in himself, adding, 'You turned Your face away from me, and I was troubled.' Yet he does not despair in his trouble, but prays to the Lord more earnestly, saying, 'To You, O Lord, will I cry, and will make my supplication to my God.' At length, he received the answer to his prayer, and bears witness that he was heard, saying, 'The Lord has heard and taken pity on me; the Lord has become my helper.' But in what way? 'You have turned my mourning into joy,' he said, 'and have surrounded me with

1. Ps. xxx, 6.

gladness.' If this is the experience of great Saints, it is not for us, poor and frail as we are, to despair if we are sometimes fervent and sometimes cold of heart. The Holy Spirit comes and goes, according to His good pleasure; therefore holy Job says, 'You visit him early in the morning, and suddenly You chasten him.'[1]

In what, then, can I place my hope or trust, save in the great mercy of God alone, and in the hope of His heavenly grace?[2] For whether I enjoy the company of good men, or devout Brethren, or faithful friends; whether holy books, beautiful treatises, or sweet singing and hymns; all these are of little help or comfort when I am forsaken by grace and left to my own poverty. At such a time there is no better remedy than patience and submission to the will of God.

I have never found anyone, however religious and devout, who did not sometimes experience withdrawal of grace, or feel a lessening of devotion. And no Saint has ever lived, however highly rapt and enlightened, who did not suffer temptation sooner or later. For he is not worthy of high contemplation who has not suffered some trials for God's sake. Indeed, the temptation that precedes is often a sign of comfort to follow. For heavenly comfort is promised to those who have been tried and tempted. 'To him who overcomes,' says God, 'I will give to eat of the Tree of Life.'[3]

Divine comfort is granted that a man may be the stronger to endure adversity; and temptation follows, lest he become proud of his virtue. The Devil never sleeps, nor is the flesh yet dead; never cease, therefore, to prepare yourself for battle against the unresting enemies who lie in wait for you on all sides.

1. Job vii, 18.   2. Ps. li, 10.   3. Rev. ii, 7.

CHAPTER 10

On Gratitude for God's Grace

WHY do you look for rest, since you are born to work? Dispose yourself to patience rather than comfort, and to the carrying of the cross rather than pleasure. What man of the world would not gladly receive spiritual comfort and joy, if he were sure of retaining it? For spiritual comfort surpasses all worldly delights and bodily pleasures. All worldly pleasures are either vain or unseemly; spiritual joys alone are pleasant and honourable, for they spring from virtue, and are infused by God into the pure of heart. But no man may enjoy these heavenly consolations at will, for temptations are seldom absent for long.

False liberty of mind and overweening self-confidence are a great hindrance to heavenly visitations. God is generous in granting us the grace of comfort; but man does ill in not returning all to God with gratitude. This is why His gifts of grace cannot flow freely in us, because we are ungrateful to the Giver, and do not return them to their Fount and Source. God will always give grace to those who are grateful, but what He grants to the humble is withheld from the proud.

I desire no consolation that would deprive me of contrition, nor do I aspire to any contemplation that might lead me to pride. For not all that is high is holy; nor all that is pleasant, good; nor every desire pure; nor is all that is dear to us pleasing to God. I gladly accept that grace which makes me ever more humble, more reverent, and more ready to renounce self. For whoever is taught by the gift of grace and chastened by its withdrawal will not presume to attribute any good to himself, but will acknowledge himself poor and devoid of virtue. Render to God whatever is God's,[1] and attribute to

1. Matt. xxii, 21.

yourself whatever is yours; that is, give thanks to God for His grace, and confess that the guilt and penalty of sin are yours alone.

Set yourself always in the lowest place,[1] and you shall be awarded the highest; for the highest cannot stand without the lowest. The Saints stand highest in God's eyes who are lowest in their own; and the more glorious they are, the more humble is their spirit. Filled with truth and heavenly glory, they have no desire for vain glory. Grounded and established in God, they cannot be proud. They ascribe all goodness to God; they seek no glory from one another, but the glory which comes from God alone.[2] They desire above all things, and strive always, that God be praised in themselves and in all His Saints.

Be thankful for the smallest blessing, and you will deserve to receive greater. Value the least gifts no less than the greatest, and simple graces as especial favours. If you remember the dignity of the Giver, no gift will seem small or mean, for nothing can be valueless that is given by the most high God. Even if He awards punishment and pain, accept them gladly, for whatever He allows to befall us is always for our salvation. Let whoever desires to retain the grace of God be thankful for the grace given him, and be patient when it is withdrawn. Let him pray for its return, and let him be prudent and humble lest he lose it once more.

1. Luke xiv, 10.   2. John v, 44.

On the Few Lovers of the Cross of Jesus

JESUS has many who love His Kingdom in Heaven, but few who bear His Cross.[1] He has many who desire comfort, but few who desire suffering. He finds many to share His feast, but few His fasting. All desire to rejoice with Him, but few are willing to suffer for His sake. Many follow Jesus to the Breaking of Bread, but few to the drinking of the Cup of His Passion. Many admire His miracles, but few follow Him in the humiliation of His Cross. Many love Jesus as long as no hardship touches them. Many praise and bless Him, as long as they are receiving any comfort from Him. But if Jesus withdraw Himself, they fall to complaining and utter dejection.

They who love Jesus for His own sake, and not for the sake of comfort for themselves, bless Him in every trial and anguish of heart, no less than in the greatest joy. And were He never willing to bestow comfort on them, they would still always praise Him and give Him thanks.

Oh, how powerful is the pure love of Jesus, free from all self-interest and self-love! Are they not all mercenary, who are always seeking comfort? Do they not betray themselves as lovers of self rather than of Christ, when they are always thinking of their own advantage and gain? Where will you find one who is willing to serve God without reward?

Seldom is anyone so spiritual as to strip himself entirely of self-love. Who can point out anyone who is truly poor in spirit and entirely detached from creatures? His rare worth exceeds all on earth. If a man gave away all that he possessed, yet it is nothing. And if he did hard penance, still it is little. And if he attained all knowledge, he is still far from his goal. And if he had great virtue and most ardent devotion, he still lacks much, and especially the 'one thing needful to him'.[2]

1. Luke xiv, 27.   2. Luke x, 42.

And what is this? That he forsake himself and all else, and completely deny himself, retaining no trace of self-love. And when he has done all that he ought to do, let him feel that he has done nothing.

Let him not regard as great what others might esteem great, but let him truthfully confess himself an unprofitable servant. For these are the words of the Truth Himself: 'When you shall have done all those things that are commanded you, say, "We are unprofitable servants".'[1] Then he may indeed be called poor and naked in spirit, and say with the Prophet, 'I am alone and poor'.[2] Yet there is no man richer, more powerful or more free than he who can forsake himself and all else, and set himself in the lowest place.

CHAPTER 12

On the Royal Road of the Holy Cross

'DENY yourself, take up your cross, and follow Me.'[3] To many this saying of Jesus seems hard. But how much harder will it be to hear that word of doom, 'Depart from Me, you cursed, into everlasting fire'.[4] For those who now cheerfully hear and obey the word of the Cross[5] will not tremble to hear the sentence of eternal damnation. The sign of the Cross will appear in the heavens, when Our Lord comes as Judge. Then will all the servants of the Cross, who in their lives conformed themselves to the Crucified,[6] stand with confidence before Christ their Judge.

Why, then, do you fear to take up the Cross, which is the road to the Kingdom? In the Cross is salvation; in the Cross is life; in the Cross is protection against our enemies; in the Cross is infusion of heavenly sweetness; in the Cross is strength of

1. Luke xvii, 10.   3. Matt. xvi, 24.   5. 1 Cor. i, 18.
2. Ps. xxv, 16.   4. Matt. xxv, 41.   6. Rom. viii, 29.

mind; in the Cross is joy of spirit; in the Cross is excellence of virtue; in the Cross is perfection of holiness. There is no salvation of soul, nor hope of eternal life, save in the Cross. Take up the Cross, therefore, and follow Jesus,[1] and go forward into eternal life.[2] Christ has gone before you, bearing His Cross;[3] He died for you on the Cross, that you also may bear your cross, and desire to die on the cross with Him. For if you die with Him, you will also live with Him.[4] And if you share His sufferings, you will also share His glory.

See how in the Cross all things consist, and in dying on it all things depend. There is no other way to life and to true inner peace, than the way of the Cross, and of daily self-denial. Go where you will, seek what you will; you will find no higher way above nor safer way below than the road of the Holy Cross. Arrange and order all things to your own ideas and wishes, yet you will still find suffering to endure, whether you will or not; so you will always find the Cross. For you will either endure bodily pain, or suffer anguish of mind and spirit.

At times, God will withdraw from you; at times you will be troubled by your neighbour, and, what is more, you will often be a burden to yourself. Neither can any remedy or comfort bring you relief, but you must bear it as long as God wills. For God desires that you learn to bear trials without comfort, that you may yield yourself wholly to Him, and grow more humble through tribulation. No man feels so deeply in his heart the Passion of Christ as he who has to suffer in like manner. The Cross always stands ready, and everywhere awaits you. You cannot escape it, wherever you flee; for wherever you go, you bear yourself, and always find yourself. Look up or down, without you or within, and everywhere you will find the Cross. And everywhere you must

1. Matt. xvi, 24.   3. John xix, 17.
2. Matt. xxv, 46.   4. Rom. vi, 8.

have patience, if you wish to attain inner peace, and win an eternal crown.

If you bear the cross willingly, it will bear you and lead you to your desired goal, where pain shall be no more; but it will not be in this life. If you bear the cross unwillingly, you make it a burden, and load yourself more heavily; but you must needs bear it. If you cast away one cross, you will certainly find another, and perhaps a heavier.

Do you think to escape what no mortal man has been able to escape? Which of the Saints lived without cross or trial? Even our Lord Jesus Christ was never without sorrow and pain, as long as He lived. 'Christ must needs suffer,' said He, 'and rise again from the dead, and so enter into His glory.'[1] Why, then, do you seek any other road than this royal road of the Holy Cross? The whole life of Christ was a cross and martyrdom; and do you look for rest and selfish pleasure?

You are greatly mistaken if you look for anything save to endure trials, for all this mortal life is full of troubles,[2] and everywhere marked with crosses. The further a man advances in the spiritual life, the heavier and more numerous he finds the crosses, for his ever-deepening love of God makes more bitter the sorrows of his earthly exile.

Yet a man who is afflicted in many ways is not without solace and comfort, for he perceives the great benefit to be reaped from the bearing of his cross. For while he bears it with a good will, the whole burden is changed into hope of God's comfort. And the more the body is subdued by affliction, the more is the spirit strengthened by grace within. Sometimes he is so greatly comforted by the desire to suffer adversity for love of conforming to the Cross of Christ, that he would not wish to be without grief and pain;[3] for he knows that the more he can suffer for His sake, the more pleasing he will be to God. This desire does not spring from man's own

1. Luke xxiv, 26.　　　2. Job xiv, 1.　　　3. 2 Cor. iv, 10.

86

strength, but from the grace of Christ, which can and does effect such great things in the frail frame of man; so that which nature fears and avoids, he boldly meets and loves through ardour of spirit.

Man is not by nature inclined to carry the cross, to love the cross, to chasten the body, and bring it into subjection;[1] to refuse honours, to submit to insults with goodwill, to despise himself and welcome disparagement; to bear all adversity and loss, and to desire no kind of prosperity in this world. And if you trust in your own strength, you will be unable to achieve any of these things. But if you trust in the Lord, you will be given strength from Heaven, and the world and the flesh will become subject to your will. Neither will you fear your enemy the Devil, if you are armed with faith and signed with the Cross of Christ.

Resolve, then, as a good and faithful servant of Christ, manfully to bear the cross of your Lord, who was crucified for love of you. Prepare yourself to endure many trials and obstacles in this vale of tears; for such will be your lot wherever you are, and you will encounter them wherever you conceal yourself. It must needs be so; nor is there any remedy or means of escape from ills and griefs; you must endure them. Drink lovingly the cup of your Lord,[2] if you wish to be His friend, and to share all with Him. Leave consolations to God, to dispose as He wills. But set yourself to endure trials, regarding them as the greatest of all comforts, 'for the sufferings of this present time are not worthy to be compared with the glory to come',[3] even though you alone were to endure them all.

When you have arrived at that state when trouble seems sweet and acceptable to you for Christ's sake, then all is well with you, for you have found paradise upon earth. But so long as suffering is grievous to you and you seek to escape it,

1. 1 Cor. ix, 27.   2. Matt. xx, 23.   3. Rom. viii, 18.

so long will it go ill with you, for the trouble you try to escape will pursue you everywhere.

If you steel yourself – as you must – to suffer and to die, all will go better with you, and you will find peace. For although, like Saint Paul, you were 'caught up into the third heaven',[1] you would not on this account be secured against suffering further adversity. For Jesus says, 'I will show him how great things he must suffer for My Name.'[2] Therefore, be prepared to suffer, if you wish to love Jesus and serve Him for ever.

Oh, if only you were worthy to suffer for the Name of Jesus! How great and enduring a glory would be yours! How great would be the joy of the Saints of God! How edified your friends would be! For all men commend patience, although few are willing to suffer. It is right that you should suffer a little for the sake of Christ, since many suffer greater things for worldly motives.

Be assured of this, that you must live a dying life. And the more completely a man dies to self, the more he begins to live to God.[3] No man is fit to understand heavenly things, unless he is resigned to bear hardships for Christ's sake. Nothing is more acceptable to God, and nothing more salutary for yourself, than to suffer gladly for Christ's sake. And if it lies in your choice, you should choose rather to suffer hardships for Christ's sake, than to be refreshed by many consolations; for thus you will more closely resemble Christ and all His Saints. For our merit and spiritual progress does not consist in enjoying such sweetness and consolation, but rather in the bearing of great burdens and troubles.

Had there been a better way, more profitable to the salvation of mankind than suffering, then Christ would have revealed it in His word and life. But He clearly urges both His own disciples and all who wish to follow Him to carry the

1. 2 Cor. xii, 4.   3. Rom. vi, 9.
2. Acts ix, 16.

cross, saying, 'If any will come after Me, let him deny himself, and take up his cross and follow Me.'[1] Therefore, when we have read and studied all things, let this be our final resolve: 'that through much tribulation we must enter the Kingdom of God.'[2]

1. Mark viii, 34.   2. Acts xiv, 22.

BOOK THREE

ON INWARD CONSOLATION

CHAPTER I
How Christ Speaks Inwardly to the Soul

'I WILL hear what the Lord God speaks within me.'[1] Blessed is the soul that hears the Lord speaking within it,[2] and receives comfort from His Word. Blessed are the ears that hear the still, small voice of God,[3] and disregard the whispers of the world. Blessed are the ears that listen to Truth teaching inwardly, and not to the voices of the world. Blessed are the eyes that are closed to outward things, but are open to inward things. Blessed are those who enter deeply into inner things, and daily prepare themselves to receive the secrets of heaven. Blessed are those who strive to devote themselves wholly to God, and free themselves from all the entanglements of the world. Consider these things, O my soul, and shut fast the doors against the desires of the senses, that you may hear what the Lord your God speaks within you.

Your Beloved says: 'I am your Salvation,[4] your Peace, and your Life; keep close to Me, and you shall find peace.' Set aside the things of time, and seek those of eternity; for what are the things of time but deceits? And how can any creature help you, if your Creator abandon you? Set aside, therefore, all else, and make yourself acceptable to your Creator, and be faithful to Him, that you may lay hold on true blessedness.

1. Ps. lxxxv, 8.	3. 1 Kings xix, 12.
2. 1 Sam. iii, 9.	4. Ps. xxxv, 3.

How Truth Instructs us in Silence

THE DISCIPLE. 'Speak, Lord, for Your servant listens.'[1] 'I am Your servant; grant me understanding, that I may know Your testimonies.'[2] 'Incline my heart to the words of Your mouth;[3] let Your speech descend on me like the dew.'[4] The people of Israel of old time said to Moses, 'Speak with us, and we will hear: let not God speak with us, lest we die.'[5] But I do not pray thus, O Lord; but with the Prophet Samuel, I humbly and earnestly beg, 'Speak, Lord, for your servant listens.' Let not Moses or any of the Prophets speak to me, but rather do You speak, O Lord God, who inspire and enlighten the Prophets. You alone can perfectly instruct me without their aid, but without You they can do nothing.

The Prophets can preach the word, but they cannot bestow the Spirit. They speak most eloquently, but if You are silent, they cannot fire the heart. They instruct in the letter, but You open the understanding. They set forth the mysteries, but You reveal the meaning of all secrets. They teach your commandments, but You help us to observe them. They point the way, but You grant us strength to follow it. Their action is external; You instruct and enlighten the heart. They water the seed; You make it fruitful.[6] They proclaim the words, but You impart understanding to the mind.

Therefore, let not Moses speak to me, but You, O Lord my God, the Everlasting Truth, lest I die and bear no fruit if I am but warned in word, and not kindled at heart; lest it turn to my condemnation, if I hear Your word, but do not obey it; know it, but do not love it; believe it, but do not

1. 1 Sam. iii, 9.	3. Ps. lxxviii, 1.	5. Exod. xx, 19.
2. Ps. cxix, 125.	4. Deut. xxxii, 2.	6. 1 Cor. iii, 7.

keep it. Therefore, speak, Lord, for Your servant is listening. 'You have the words of eternal life.'[1] Speak to me, Lord, and comfort my soul: order my life to Your praise, glory, and eternal honour.

CHAPTER 3

On Humble Attention to God's Word

CHRIST. My son, hear My words. They are of surpassing sweetness, and excel all the learning of the philosophers and wise men of this world. My words are spirit and life,[2] not to be weighed by man's understanding. They are not to be quoted for vain pleasure, but are to be heard in silence,[3] and received with all humility and love.

THE DISCIPLE. Blessed is the man whom you instruct, O Lord, and teach him out of Your Law. You refresh him in evil days,[4] and he will not be desolate on the earth.

CHRIST. I have taught the Prophets from the beginning of the world,[5] and I do not cease to speak to all men today; but many are hardened, and deaf to My voice. Many listen more willingly to the world than to God, and would rather follow the desires of the body than the good pleasure of God. The world promises passing rewards of little worth, and is served with great eagerness; I promise eternal and rich rewards, yet the hearts of men are indifferent to them. Who is there who serves and obeys Me with as great devotion as he serves the world and its rulers? 'Be ashamed, O Sidon,'[6] cries the sea; and if you ask the reason, hear why.

For a small reward a man will hurry away on a long journey, while for eternal life many will hardly take a single

1. John vi, 68.   3. Eccles. ix, 17.   5. Heb. i, 1.
2. John vi, 63.   4. Ps. xciv, 13.   6. Isa. xxiii, 4.

step. Men seek petty gains; they will quarrel shamefully over a single coin; for a mere trifle or vague promise they will toil day and night. Oh, the shame of it! For an imperishable good, for a reward beyond all reckoning, for the highest honour and for glory without end, they are unwilling to endure a little toil. O unwilling and complaining servant, shame on you that worldly men are more ready for damnation than you for salvation; for they are more wholehearted in vanity than you in the Truth. They are often deceived in their hopes, but no one is ever deceived in My promises, and I never send away empty any who trusts in Me. What I promise, I give; what I have said, I will perform, provided you remain faithful in My lord to the end. I am the rewarder of all good men, and the mighty vindicator of all the faithful.

Write My words in your heart, and meditate on them earnestly; they will aid you in temptation. Whatever you do not understand when you read, you shall know in the day of My coming. I visit My chosen in two ways; with trial and with consolation. Day by day, I teach them two lessons, one in which I correct their faults, and the other in which I encourage them to progress in virtue. 'He who hears My words and despises them has One who will judge him on the Last Day.'[1]

A Prayer for the Grace of Devotion

THE DISCIPLE. O Lord my God, You are my all and every good. And what am I, that I should presume to address You?[2] I am the poorest of Your servants and a wretched worm, far more poor and worthless than I can ever realize or express. Yet, Lord, remember that I am nothing: I have nothing, and can do nothing.[3] You alone are good, just

1. John xii, 48. 2. Gen. xviii, 27. 3. 2 Cor. xii, 10.

and holy; You can do all things, fill all things,[1] bestow all things, leaving only the wicked empty-handed. Remember Your mercies,[2] Lord, and fill my heart with Your grace, since it is Your will that none of Your works should be worthless. How can I endure this life of sorrows, unless You strengthen me with Your mercy and grace? Do not turn Your face from me;[3] do not delay Your coming, nor withdraw Your consolation from me, lest my soul become like a waterless desert.[4] Teach me, O Lord, to do Your will;[5] teach me to live worthily and humbly in Your sight; for You are my Wisdom, who know me truly, and who knew me before the world was made, and before I had my being.

CHAPTER 4
On Truth and Humility

CHRIST. My son, walk before Me in truth, and constantly seek Me in simplicity of heart.[6] He who walks before Me in truth shall be protected against the assaults of evil; truth shall deliver him from his deceivers and from the slanders of the wicked. If truth set you free,[7] you are truly free, and need care nothing for the vain words of men.

THE DISCIPLE. Lord, this is true; let it be as you have said. Let Your truth be my teacher and my guard, and lead me to salvation in the end. Let it free me from every evil affection and lawless love, and I will walk before You in complete freedom of heart.

CHRIST. I will teach you, says the Truth, what is pleasing to Me.[8] Remember your sins with deep sorrow and displeasure, and never think yourself to be anything because of your

1. Job xlii, 2.
2. Ps. xxv, 6.
3. Ps. li, 1; cxliii, 7.
4. Ps. cxliii, 6.
5. Ps. cxliii, 10.
6. Gen. xvii, 1.
7. John viii, 32.
8. 1 John iii, 22.

good deeds. Remember that you are a sinner, entangled and enchained by many passions. Of yourself, you always tend to nothing; you quickly fail, and are overcome; you are soon disturbed and overthrown. You have nothing of which to boast, but many things of which to be ashamed, for you are much weaker than you realize.

Let nothing that you have achieved seem of great importance. Let nothing seem great, precious or admirable to you; nothing worthy of regard, nothing high, praiseworthy or desirable, save that which is everlasting. Let the eternal Truth be your sole and supreme joy, and let your own deep unworthiness always distress you. Nothing should be more feared, condemned, and shunned than your own sins and vices; these should cause you more distress than the loss of everything. Some do not live sincerely in My sight,[1] but, moved by curiosity and conceit, wish to know My secrets and to fathom the high mysteries of God, while neglecting the salvation of their own souls. When I refuse them, such men often fall into great temptations and sins through pride and curiosity.

Stand in awe of God's judgement,[2] and fear the anger of Almighty God.[3] Do not presume to investigate the ways of the Most High, but rather examine yourself, see how greatly you have sinned, and how much good you have left undone. Some carry their devotion only in books, pictures, and other visible signs and representations. Some have Me on their lips, but seldom in their hearts.[4] There are others who are enlightened in mind and pure in affection, who long always for the things of heaven. These listen with reluctance to worldly matters, and grudge even to serve their bodily needs. They fully understand what the Spirit of Truth speaks

1. Tob. iii, 5.   3. 2 Macc. vii, 38.
2. Ps. cxix, 120.   4. Isa. xxix, 13.

within them.[1] For He teaches them to despise earthly things and to love heavenly; to forsake this world, and to long for Heaven.

CHAPTER 5
On the Wonderful Effect of Divine Love

THE DISCIPLE. O Heavenly Father, Father of my Lord Jesus Christ, blessed be Your Name for ever, for You have deigned to consider me, the poorest of Your servants. Father of mercies and God of all comfort,[2] I thank You that, unworthy as I am, You sometimes refresh me with Your consolation. Blessing and glory to You, with Your sole-begotten Son and with the Holy Spirit the Comforter, now and through endless ages. You are my glory,[3] and the joy of my heart;[4] for You are my hope, and my refuge in time of trouble.[5]

As yet my love is weak, and my virtue imperfect, and I have great need of Your strength and comfort. Therefore, visit me often, I pray, and instruct me in Your holy laws. Set me free from evil passions, and heal my heart from all disorderly affections; that, healed and cleansed in spirit, I may grow able to love, strong to endure, and steadfast to persevere.

Love is a mighty power, a great and complete good; Love alone lightens every burden, and makes the rough places smooth. It bears every hardship as though it were nothing, and renders all bitterness sweet and acceptable. The love of Jesus is noble, and inspires us to great deeds; it moves us always to desire perfection. Love aspires to high things, and is held back by nothing base. Love longs to be free, a stranger to every worldly desire, lest its inner vision become

1. Matt. x, 20; John   2. 2 Cor. i, 3.   4. Ps. cxix, 111.
    xvi, 13.   3. Ps. iii, 3.   5. Ps. lix, 16.

dimmed, and lest worldly self-interest hinder it or ill-fortune cast it down. Nothing is sweeter than love, nothing stronger, nothing higher, nothing wider, nothing more pleasant, nothing fuller or better in heaven or earth; for love is born of God,[1] and can rest only in God, above all created things.

Love flies, runs, and leaps for joy; it is free and unrestrained. Love gives all for all, resting in One who is highest above all things, from whom every good flows and proceeds. Love does not regard the gifts, but turns to the Giver of all good gifts. Love knows no limits, but ardently transcends all bounds. Love feels no burden, takes no account of toil, attempts things beyond its strength; love sees nothing as impossible, for it feels able to achieve all things. Love therefore does great things; it is strange and effective; while he who lacks love faints and fails.

Love is watchful, and while resting, never sleeps; weary, it is never exhausted; imprisoned, it is never in bonds; alarmed, it is never afraid; like a living flame and a burning torch, it surges upward and surely surmounts every obstacle. Whoever loves God knows well the sound of His voice. A loud cry in the ears of God is that burning love of the soul which exclaims, 'My God and my love, You are all mine, and I am Yours.'

A Prayer

Deepen Your love in me, O Lord, that I may learn in my inmost heart how sweet it is to love, to be dissolved, and to plunge myself into Your love. Let Your love possess and raise me above myself, with a fervour and wonder beyond imagination. Let me sing the song of love.[2] Let me follow You, my Beloved, into the heights. Let my soul spend itself in Your praise, rejoicing for love. Let me love You more

1. 1 John iv, 7.   2. Isa. v, 1.

than myself, and myself only for Your own sake. Let me love all men who truly love You, as the law of love commands, which shines out from You.

Love is swift, pure, tender, joyful, and pleasant. Love is strong, patient, faithful, prudent, long-suffering, vigorous, and never self-seeking.[1] For when a man is self-seeking he abandons love. Love is watchful, humble, and upright; Love is not fickle and sentimental, nor is it intent on vanities. It is sober, pure, steadfast, quiet, and guarded in all the senses. Love is submissive and obedient to superiors, mean and contemptible in its own sight, devoted and thankful to God, trusting and hoping in Him even when not enjoying His sweetness; for none can live in love without suffering.

Whoever is not prepared to endure everything, and to stand firmly by the will of the Beloved, is not worthy to be called a lover. A lover must willingly accept every hardship and bitterness for the sake of his Beloved, and must never desert Him because of adversity.

CHAPTER 6
On the Proof of a True Lover

CHRIST. My son, you are not yet a brave and wise lover.

THE DISCIPLE. Why, Lord?

CHRIST. Because as soon as you encounter a little trouble, you abandon what you have begun, and eagerly seek for comfort. A brave lover stands firm in temptation, and pays no heed to the crafty arguments of the Devil. He is as true to Me in trouble as in prosperity.[2]

A wise lover values not so much the gift of the lover, as the love of the giver. He esteems the affection above the gift, and values every gift far below the Beloved. A noble

1. I. Cor. xiii, 4.   2. Phil. iv, 12.

99

lover is not content with a gift, but desires Myself above all gifts. All is not lost, therefore, if sometimes you do not feel that devotion to Me and My Saints that you desire. The good and pleasant affection which you sometimes enjoy is the effect of My grace in you, and is a foretaste of your heavenly home; but do not rely on it too much, for it comes and goes. To fight against evil thoughts as they occur, and to reject with scorn the suggestions of the Devil, is a noteworthy sign of virtue and merit.

Let no strange fancies disturb you, from whatever source they spring. Hold to your purpose bravely, and keep an upright intent towards God. It is no illusion if you are sometimes rapt out of yourself, yet swiftly return to the usual trivial thoughts of men. For these are involuntary rather than deliberate, and as long as they do not please you, can be turned to your gain and not your loss.

You may be sure that the old Enemy is working by every means to frustrate your desire for good, and to entice you away from every spiritual exercise of devotion; from veneration of the Saints, from devout meditation on My Passion, from profitable examination of your sins, from the guard of your heart, and from the firm resolve to grow in holiness. He suggests many evil thoughts to discourage you, and to draw you away from holy reading and prayer. Humble Confession is hateful to him, and if he could, he would make you give up Communion. Do not listen to him or believe him, however often he tries to entrap you. Charge him with it, when he suggests evil and unholy things. Say to him, 'Away, unclean spirit![1] Blush for shame, wretch! You are foul indeed to speak of these things! Off with you, most evil of liars! You shall have no part in me. Jesus will be with me like a mighty warrior, and you will stand confounded.[2] I would rather die and suffer any

1. Matt. iv, 10. 2. Jer. xx, 11.

torture than consent to you. Be silent, and shut your mouth! I will listen to you no longer, however often you pester me.' 'The Lord is my light and my salvation: whom shall I fear?'[1] 'Though a host should encamp against me, my heart shall not be afraid.'[2] 'The Lord is my helper and redeemer.'[3]

Give battle, like a good soldier,[4] and if through weakness you sometimes fall, take greater strength than before and put your trust in My more abundant grace. Be also on your guard against vain complacency and conceit, for this leads many into error, and causes almost incurable blindness of heart. Let the overthrow of the proud, who presumed in their own strength, be a warning to you and keep you always humble.

CHAPTER 7
On Concealing Grace under Humility

CHRIST. My son, it is safer and better for you to conceal the grace of devotion; do not boast of it, do not speak much of it, and do not dwell much on it. It is better to think the more humbly of yourself, and to fear that this grace has been granted to one who is unworthy of it. Never depend too much on these feelings, for they may be rapidly changed to the opposite. When you enjoy such grace, consider how sad and needy you are without it. Progress in the spiritual life consists not so much in enjoying the grace of consolation, as in bearing its withdrawal with humility, resignation and patience, neither growing weary in prayer nor neglecting your other acts of devotion. Do willingly, and to the best of your ability and understanding, whatever lies in your power,

1. Ps. xxvii, 1.   3. Ps. xix, 14.
2. Ps. xxvii, 3.   4. 2 Tim. ii, 3.

and do not neglect your spiritual life because of any dryness or anxiety of mind.

There are many who grow impatient or indolent when all does not go according to their wishes. But man's life is not always in his control;[1] it belongs to God alone to give and to comfort when He wills, as much as He wills, and whom He wills, just as He pleases and no more. Some people, lacking discretion, have brought ruin on themselves through the grace of devotion, attempting more than lay in their power, ignoring the measure of their own littleness, and following the promptings of the heart rather than the dictates of reason. And because they presumed to greater things than pleased God, they soon lost His grace. These souls, who aspired to build their nest in Heaven,[2] became needy and wretched outcasts, in order that, through humiliation and poverty, they might learn not to fly with their own wings, but to trust themselves under My wings.[3] For those who are still new and untried in the Way of the Lord can easily be deceived and lost, unless they are guided by wise counsel.

If they follow their own notions rather than trust others of proved experience, their end will be perilous unless they are willing to be drawn away from their own conceit. Those who are wise in their own conceit seldom humbly accept guidance from others. A little knowledge and understanding tempered by humility is better than a great store of learning coupled with vain complacency. It is better to have few talents than many of which you might be conceited. Whoever yields himself to joy, forgetful of his former poverty, is very unwise, for he forgets also that pure reverence for the Lord which fears to lose grace already given. Nor is he wise who, in trouble and adversity, yields to despair, and fails to put his trust in Me.

1. Jer. x, 23.   2. Isa. xiv, 13.   3. Ps. xci, 4.

The man who feels secure in time of peace, will often in time of war be found discouraged and afraid. If you were careful to remain always humble and modest in your own esteem, and to direct and control your mind rightly,[1] you would not fall so readily into danger and disgrace. It is good advice, that when the spirit of devotion is aflame in your heart, you should consider how you will fare when the light leaves you. When this happens, remember that this light will one day return, which I have now for a while withdrawn[2] as a warning to you and for My glory.

Such a trial is often more profitable than if all went agreeably with you, and in accordance with your wishes. For a man's merit is not to be reckoned by the visions and comforts he may enjoy, nor by his learning in the Scriptures, nor by his being raised to high dignity. Rather is it by his being grounded in humility and filled with divine love; by his pure, constant, and sincere seeking of God's glory; by his low esteem and honest depreciation of himself;[3] and by his preference for humiliation and despite rather than honours at the hands of men.

CHAPTER 8

On Humility in the Sight of God

THE DISCIPLE. I will presume to speak to my Lord, though I am but dust and ashes.[4] If I esteem myself to be anything more, You confront me, and my sins bear a true witness against me, that I cannot contradict. But if I humble myself and acknowledge my nothingness; if I cast away all my self-esteem and reduce myself to the dust that I really am, then Your grace will come to me, and Your light will enter my

1. James iv, 6.   3. Ps. xv, 4.
2. Job. vii, 19; Ps. xiii, 1.   4. Gen. xviii, 27.

heart; thus will the last trace of self-esteem be engulfed in the depth of my own nothingness, and perish for ever. Thus You show me my true self, what I am, what I have been, and what I have become; for I am nothing, and did not know it. By myself I am nothing, and am all weakness. But if for a moment You look on me, I become strong once again, and am filled with new joy. It amazes me how speedily You raise and enfold me with Your grace, who of myself ever fall into the depths.

It is Your love that achieves this, freely guiding and supporting me in my many needs, guarding me from grievous perils, and, as I may truthfully confess, rescuing me from evils without number. And whereas by perverse self-love I had lost myself,[1] now by lovingly seeking You alone, I have found both myself and You; for by that love I have humbled myself to utter nothingness. Dearest Lord, You deal with me above my deserts, and above all I dare hope or pray for.

O Blessed Lord God, I am not worthy of any blessings, yet Your generosity and infinite goodness never cease to benefit even those who are ungrateful,[2] and have wandered far from You. O turn our hearts to You,[3] that we may be thankful, humble and devoted; for You are our Salvation, our Power, and our Strength.

CHAPTER 9

How God Alone is our True End

CHRIST. My son, I must be your supreme and final End, if you desire true happiness. Fixed on Myself, your affection which too often is wrongly inclined to yourself and creatures, will be cleansed. For whenever you seek yourself, at once you become discouraged and desolate. Therefore,

1. John xii, 25.   2. Matt. v, 45.   3. Ps. lxxx, 19.

refer all things to Me, for it is I who have given all to you. Consider everything as springing from the supreme Good,[1] since to Myself, as their Source, must all things return.

From Myself, as from a living fountain, both small and great, rich and poor alike draw the water of life;[2] and they who freely and willingly serve Me, shall receive grace upon grace. But whoever desires to glory in anything outside Me,[3] or to delight in some personal good thing, will not be established in true joy, nor uplifted in heart,[4] but will be hindered and frustrated in countless ways. Therefore, ascribe no good to yourself, nor to any man, but ascribe all to God, without whom man has nothing. I have given all, and it is My will that all return to Me again; I shall require a grateful and exact account.

This, then, is the truth, by which vainglory is put to flight. And if heavenly grace and true charity enter in, there will be no envy or meanness of heart, nor will self-love retain possession. Divine charity overcomes everything,[5] enlarging every power of the soul. If you are truly wise, you will rejoice and hope in Me alone; for none is good but God alone,[6] who is to be praised above all, and to be blessed in all.

CHAPTER 10

On the Joy of God's Service

THE DISCIPLE. Lord, I will speak once more; I cannot remain silent. I will say to my God, my Lord and my King, who dwells on high, 'Oh, how great and manifold are Your joys, kept in secret for those who fear You.'[7] But what are You to those who love You? What to those who serve You

---

1. Ecclus, i, 5.
2. John iv, 14; Rev. xxi, 6.
3. 1 Cor. i, 29.
4. Ps. cxix, 32.
5. I Cor. xiii, 8.
6. Luke xviii, 19.
7. Ps. xxxi, 19.

with their whole heart? The contemplation of Yourself is the ineffable sweetness that You grant to those who love You. And this is the supreme manifestation of Your love, that when I had no being, You created me; when I went astray, You led me back to Your service, and taught me to love You.[1]

O Fount of eternal love, what may I say of You? How can I forget You, who have deigned to remember me, even after I was corrupted and lost? You have showed mercy on Your servant beyond all my hope; You have given grace and friendship beyond all my deserts. What return can I make to You for this grace?[2] For it is not granted to all men to forsake everything, to renounce the world, and to enter the life of religion. And is it a great thing that I should serve You, whom all creation is bound to serve? It should not seem much to me that I should serve you; rather is it great and wonderful to me that You should see fit to receive into Your service one so poor and unworthy, and count him among Your beloved servants.

All that I have is Yours, and myself with it.[3] Yet it is really You who serve me, rather than I You. Heaven and earth, which You created for the use of man, await Your pleasure, and obey Your laws day by day. And even this is little, for You have appointed the very Angels to minister to men.[4] But what surpasses all these, is that You Yourself stoop to serve man, and have promised him the gift of Yourself.

What return can I make for all these countless favours? If only I could serve You faithfully all the days of my life! If only I could render You worthy service, even for a single day! For You alone are worthy of all service, honour, and eternal praise.[5] You are truly my God, and I Your poor

1. Isa. lvii, 15.   3. 1 Cor. iv, 7.   5. Rev. iv, 11.
2. Ps. cxvi, 12.   4. Ps. xci, 11.

servant, who am bound to serve with all my powers, nor should I ever weary in Your praise. This is my wish and desire; whatever is lacking in me, I pray You to supply.

It is a great honour and glory to serve you, and to despise all else for Your sake; for great grace will be given to those who have willingly entered Your most holy service. They will discover the sweetest consolations of the Holy Spirit, who for Your love have renounced all the delights of the flesh. They will win true freedom of mind, who for Your Name's sake have entered on the narrow way,[1] and set aside all worldly interests.

O gracious and joyful service of God, in which man is made truly free and holy! O sacred state of religious service, which makes man the equal of Angels, pleasing to God, terrible to devils, and an example to all the faithful! O most lovely and desirable service, in which we receive the reward of the supreme Good, and obtain the joy that abides for ever!

CHAPTER II
On Control of the Heart

CHRIST. My son, you have still many things to learn.

THE DISCIPLE. What are these, Lord?

CHRIST. How you must frame your desires in accordance with My good pleasure,[2] and be not a lover of self, but an earnest follower of My will. Desires often inflame you and drive you violently onwards; but consider whether it be My honour or self-interest that moves you most. If I Myself be the cause, you will be content with whatever I shall determine; but if self-interest is your hidden motive, this will be a hindrance and burden to you.

1. Matt. vii, 14.   2. Matt. vi, 10.

Take care, therefore, not to rely overmuch on any preconceived desire without asking My counsel, lest you regret or become displeased at what first pleased you, and for which you were eager. For not every feeling that seems good is at once to be acted upon, nor is every feeling that runs contrary to your inclinations to be immediately rejected. It is sometimes necessary to restrain even your good intentions and endeavours, lest by over-eagerness your mind becomes distracted; lest by lack of discipline you cause offence to others; or lest you suddenly become confused and upset by the opposition of others.

You must bravely and forcibly resist your sensual appetite, taking no account of what the body likes or dislikes, and struggle to subdue the unwilling flesh to the spirit.[1] For it must be corrected and brought under control, until it is obedient in everything. It must learn to be content with little, to take pleasure in simple things, and not to complain at any hardship.

CHAPTER 12
On Learning Patience

THE DISCIPLE. O Lord God, I know that I need patience above all else,[2] for in this life there are many trials. For however earnestly I seek peace, I cannot escape struggle and sorrow.[3] CHRIST. This is true, My son. But My will is that you do not try to find a place free from temptations and troubles. Rather, seek a peace that endures even when you are beset by various temptations and tried by much adversity.[4] If you say that you cannot endure much, how will you endure the fires of Purgatory? Of two evils, always choose the lesser.

1. I Cor. ix, 27.   3. Ps. xxxi, 10.
2. Heb. x, 36.   4. James i, 2.

Endeavour patiently to endure for God's sake all the ills of this life, that you may escape eternal punishment. Do you imagine that worldly men suffer little or nothing? Ask the most wealthy, and you will not find it so.

But, you may say, they enjoy many pleasures, and follow their own desires; in this way they make light of any troubles. Yet, even if they enjoy whatever they desire, how long will this last? The rich of this world will vanish like smoke,[1] and no memory of their past pleasures will remain. But even in their lifetime they do not enjoy them without bitterness, weariness and fear, for the very things whence they derive their pleasures often carry with them the seeds of sorrow. And this is but just; for having sought and followed pleasures to excess, they may not enjoy them without shame and bitterness. Ah, how short-lived and false, how disorderly and base are all these pleasures! Yet so besotted and blind are such persons that, like dumb beasts, they bring death to their souls for the trivial enjoyments of this corruptible life! My son, do not follow your lusts, and do not be self-willed.[2] Delight in the Lord, and he will grant your heart's desire.[3]

If you would taste true pleasure and receive the fullness of My consolation, know this: that in the despising of worldly things and in the shunning of base delights shall be your blessing, and you shall win abundant consolation. The more you withdraw yourself from the comfort of creatures, the sweeter and more potent will be the consolations that you will find in Me. But you will not find these at once, or without sorrow, toil and effort. Old habits will stand in your way, but by better they will be overcome.[4] The body will complain, but by fervour of the spirit it can be disciplined.

1. Ps. lxviii, 2.   4. S. Augustine, *Con-*
2. Ecclus. xviii, 30.   *fessions,* VIII, xi, 25.
3. Ps. xxxvii, 4.

The Old Serpent[1] will goad and disturb you, but by prayer he will be put to flight; and by profitable labour you will bar the wide path by which he comes to attack you.

CHAPTER 13
On Obedience, after the Example of Christ

CHRIST. My son, whoever strives to withdraw from obedience, withdraws from grace. And he who seeks personal privileges, loses those that are common to all. When a man is unwilling to submit freely and willingly to his superior, it is a sign that his lower nature is not yet under his control, but frequently rebels and complains. Therefore learn to obey your superior promptly if you wish to subdue your lower nature, for the Enemy without is sooner overcome if our inner fortress remains intact. There is no enemy more wicked or troublesome to the soul than yourself, when you are not in harmony with the Spirit, and you must have a very real scorn for self, if you are to prevail against flesh and Blood. It is because you are unwilling to yield your will to that of others, that you are still full of self-love.

Is it so hard for you, who are dust and nothingness, to subject yourself to man for God's sake, when I, the Almighty and most high, who created all things from nothing, humbly subjected Myself to man for your sake?[2] I became the humblest and least of all men, that you might overcome your pride through My humility. Learn to obey, you who are but dust; learn to humble yourself, earth and clay, and to bow yourself beneath the feet of all. Learn to curb your desires, and yield yourself to complete obedience.

Direct your anger against yourself, and let no swelling pride remain in you. Show yourself so submissive and so

1. Rev. xii, 9.   2. John xiii, 14.

humble that all men may trample over you and tread on you like the mud of the streets.[1] Vain man, what right have you to complain? What can you, an unclean sinner, answer to any who reproach you, when you have so often offended God, and so many times deserved Hell? But I have spared you,[2] for your soul was precious to Me, that you might know My love, and be ever grateful for My favour: also, that you might give yourself constantly to true obedience and humility, enduring patiently any contempt laid on you.

CHAPTER 14

On the Secret Judgements of God

THE DISCIPLE. Lord, Your judgements thunder against me. My limbs tremble and shake with fear, and my soul is horribly afraid. I stand awestruck, considering how the very heavens are not pure in Your sight.[3] And if You found wickedness even among the Angels,[4] and did not spare them,[5] what can be my fate? The very stars fall from Heaven;[6] what then can I presume, who am but dust? Men whose deeds seemed praiseworthy have fallen into the pit, and I have seen those who had been fed with the Bread of Angels[7] delighted with pigs' food.

There can be no holiness, Lord, if You withdraw Yourself. No wisdom can avail, if You cease to guide. No courage can uphold, if You cease to defend. No purity is secure, if You are not guard. No watchfulness of our own can save us, unless Your holy care protects us;[8] for if You abandon us, we sink and perish.[9] But if You visit us, we are raised up and live once more. We are unstable, unless You

1. Ps. xviii, 42.
2. Ezek. xx, 17.
3. Job xv, 15.
4. Job iv, 18.
5. 2 Peter ii, 4.
6. Rev. vi, 13.
7. Ps. lxxviii, 25.
8. Ps. cxxvii, 1.
9. Matt. viii, 25.

strengthen us; we are cold and dull, unless You kindle us to fervour.

How humble and insignificant I am! If there is any good in me, it is as nothing. Lord, I submit myself in all humility to Your unfathomable judgements;[1] I acknowledge my utter nothingness. O greatness immeasurable! O sea that none can cross! Now I recognize myself as wholly and only nothing! Where now can pride lurk unseen? Where is now my former confidence in my virtue? All my empty conceit is overwhelmed in the depths of Your judgements upon me.

What is all flesh in Your sight?[2] Can the clay boast against Him who fashions it?[3] Can a man whose heart is subject to God in truth be puffed up with empty boasting?[4] The whole world cannot exalt him whom the Truth has made subject to itself, nor can he who has fixed his whole hope in God be moved by the tongues of all who flatter him. For even those who talk thus are all nothing; they will pass away with the sound of their own words, but the truth of the Lord stands fast for ever.[5]

CHAPTER 15
On the Ordering of our Desires

CHRIST. My son, let this be your constant prayer: 'Lord, if this be Your will, so let it be.[6] Lord, if this is good and profitable, give me grace to use it to Your glory. But if it be hurtful and injurious to my soul's health, then remove this desire from my mind, I pray.' Not every desire comes of the Holy Spirit, though it may seem right and good; for it is often hard to judge whether a desire springs from good or

1. Ps. xxxvi, 6.   3. Isa. xlv, 9.   5. Ps. cxvii, 2.
2. 1 Cor. i, 29.   4. Isa. xxix, 16; lxiv, 8.   6. James iv, 15.

evil motives, or whether it arises from your own inclinations. Many are deceived in the end, who at first seemed to be led by the Holy Spirit.

Whatever, therefore, the mind conceives as desirable is always to be desired and sought only in the fear of God and with a humble heart. Above all, commit all things to Me, and entrust yourself wholly to Me, saying, 'Lord, You know what is best; let everything be in accordance with Your will. Give what You will, as much as You will, and when You will. Do with me as You think good, as pleases You best, and is most to Your glory. I am in Your hand; guide me according to Your will. I am indeed Your servant,[1] and am ready for anything. I wish to live, not for myself but for You alone; how I wish I could serve You perfectly and worthily!'

A Prayer that the Will of God may be Done

THE DISCIPLE. Most kind Jesus, grant me Your grace, I pray; let it dwell in me, work in me,[2] and abide in me to the end. Grant me always to will and desire whatever is most pleasing and acceptable to You. Let Your will be mine, and let my will ever follow and be conformed wholly to Your own. Let me ever will and not will in union with Yourself, and be unable to will otherwise than You will or do not will. Grant that I may die to all things in this world, and for Your sake love to be despised and unknown. Grant me, above all else, to rest in You,[3] that my heart may find its peace in You alone; for You are the heart's true peace, its sole abiding place, and outside Yourself all is hard and restless. In this true peace that is in You, the sole, supreme, and eternal Good, I will dwell and take my rest.[4] Amen.

1. Ps. cxix, 125.   3. S. Augustine, *Conf.*, V, i.
2. Wisd. ix, 10.   4. Ps. iv, 8.

CHAPTER 16

How True Comfort is to be Sought in God Alone

THE DISCIPLE. Whatever I can wish or imagine for my consolation, I do not expect now, but hereafter. For if I were to enjoy all the pleasures of the world, and were able to taste all its delights,[1] they would surely pass away. Therefore my soul can never find full satisfaction or perfect refreshment save in God alone, who is the comfort of the poor and protector of the humble. Be patient, my soul; await the fulfilment of God's promise, and you shall enjoy the abundance of His goodness in Heaven. But if you hanker inordinately after the good things of this life, you will lose those of heaven and eternity. Therefore make right use of this world's goods, but long only for those that are eternal. This world's good things can never satisfy you, for you are not created for the enjoyment of these alone.[2]

Could you enjoy every good thing in existence, this could not of itself bring you blessing and happiness, for all true joy and blessedness rests in God alone, the Creator of all things. This happiness is not of the kind seen and admired by those who foolishly love this world, but such as is sought by the good and faithful servants of Christ, and of which the spiritual and pure in heart,[3] whose thoughts are on heaven, sometimes enjoy a foretaste. All human comfort is short-lived and empty; but blessed and true is the comfort received inwardly from the Truth. A devout man always bears Jesus his Comforter in his heart, and says to Him, 'Lord Jesus, remain with me everywhere and at all times.' Let this, then, be my comfort, to be ready and willing to forego all earthly comfort. And if Your comfort be lacking,

1. Matt. xvi, 26.
2. S. Augustine, *Sermons*, XXXVI, 6; *City of God*, XI, 25.
3. Phil. iii, 20.

may Your holy will and just trial of my life be my highest consolation; for You will not always be angry, nor will You condemn me for ever.[1]

CHAPTER 17
How we must put our Whole Trust in God

CHRIST. My son, let My will be your guide. I know what is best for you. Your mind is but human, and your judgement often influenced by personal considerations.

THE DISCIPLE. Lord, this is true, and Your providence will order my life better than I can myself: most insecure is the man who does not put all his trust in You.[2] Lord, keep my will steadfast and true to You, and do with me whatever is Your pleasure; for all is good that comes to me by Your will. If You will that darkness be my lot, blessed be Your Name; if it be light, again blessed be Your Name. If You stoop to comfort me, blessed be Your Name; and if You wish to try me, ever blessed be Your Name.

CHRIST. My son, let this be your disposition if you wish to walk with Me. Be as ready to suffer as to be glad; be as willing to be needy and poor as to enjoy wealth and plenty.

THE DISCIPLE. Lord, for Your sake I will gladly bear whatever You shall send to me. From Your hand I will accept gladly both good and ill,[3] sweet and bitter, joy and sorrow; and for all that may befall me, I will thank You. Only keep me, O Lord, from all sin, and I shall fear neither Death nor Hell.[4] Do not, I pray, reject me for ever,[5] nor blot out my name from the book of life;[6] then, whatever trials beset me can do me no harm.

1. Ps. ciii, 9; Isa. lvii, 16.
2. 1 Pet. v, 7.
3. Job ii, 10.
4. Ps. xxiii, 4.
5. Ps. lxxvii, 7.
6. Rev. iii, 5.

CHAPTER 18

How Sorrows are to be Borne Patiently

CHRIST. My son, I came down from Heaven for your salvation.[1] I took upon Myself your sorrows, not because I must, but out of pure love, that you might learn patience, and bear without complaint all the troubles of this world. From the hour of My Birth until My Death on the Cross, I had always to endure sorrow.[2] I suffered great lack of worldly goods; many accusations were levelled against Me. I bore all disgrace and insults with meekness. In return for blessings I received ingratitude; for miracles, blasphemies; for My teaching, reproofs.

THE DISCIPLE. Lord, because You were patient in Your life, in this respect especially fulfilling the command of Your Father, it is fitting that I, a wretched sinner, should bear myself patiently in accordance with Your will, and that, for the salvation of my soul, I should bear the burden of this corruptible life so long as You shall will. For though this present life is hard, yet by Your grace it is made full of merit; and by Your example and the lives of Your Saints it is rendered easier and happier for the weak. Its consolations are richer than under the old Law, when the gates of Heaven were shut, and the way thither dark, so that few cared to enter the Kingdom of Heaven. And even those who in former days were righteous and to be saved could not enter the Kingdom of Heaven until Your Passion and the Atonement of Your sacred Death.

What boundless gratitude is Your due, for revealing to me and to all faithful people the true and holy way to Your eternal Kingdom! Your life is our Way, and by holy patience we will journey onwards to You, who are our crown and consummation. If You, Lord, had not gone

1. John iii, 17.   2. Isa. liii, 3.

before us and showed the way, who could follow? How many would have stayed behind and far distant had they not Your glorious example for their guide? Even now we are cold and careless, although we have heard Your teaching and mighty acts; what would happen to us had we not Your light as our guide?[1]

CHAPTER 19

On Enduring Injuries, and the Proof of Patience

CHRIST. My son, what are you saying? Consider My sufferings and those of My Saints, and cease to complain. You have not yet shed your blood in resistance;[2] your troubles are but small in comparison with those who have suffered so much, whose temptations were so strong, whose trials so severe, and who were proved and tested in so many ways.[3] Remember the heavier sufferings of others, that you may more easily bear your own small troubles. If they do not s em small to you, beware lest your impatience be the cause; and whether they be small or great, try to bear them all patiently.

The better you prepare yourself to meet suffering, the more wisely will you act, and the greater will be your merit. You will bear all more easily if your heart and mind is diligently prepared. Do not say, 'I cannot endure such things from this person,' or, 'I will not tolerate these things: he has done me great injury, and accused me of things I never considered; from another person I might bear it, and regard it as something that must be endured.' Such thoughts are foolish, for you ignore the merit of patience and Him who rewards it, and think only of the person who has injured you and the wrong you endure.

1. John viii, 12; xii, 46.   2. Heb. xii, 4.   3. Heb. xi, 37.

You are not truly patient if you will only endure what you think fit, and only from those whom you like. A truly patient man does not consider by whom he is tried, whether by his superior, his equal, or his inferior; whether by a good and holy man, or by a perverse and wicked person. But however great or frequent the trial that besets him, and by whatever agency it comes, he accepts it gladly as from the hand of God, and counts it all gain.

Always be ready for battle if you wish for victory; you cannot win the crown of patience without a struggle;[1] if you refuse to suffer, you refuse the crown. Therefore, if you desire the crown, fight manfully and endure patiently. Without labour, no rest is won; without battle, there can be no victory.

THE DISCIPLE. Lord, make possible for me by grace what is impossible to me by nature. You know how little I can bear, and how quickly I become discouraged by a little adversity. I pray You, make every trial lovely and desirable to me for Your Name's sake, since suffering and affliction for Your sake is so profitable to the health of my soul.

CHAPTER 20

On our own Weakness, and the Trials of This Life

THE DISCIPLE. Lord, I confess my sinfulness,[2] and acknowledge my weakness. Often it is but a small matter that defeats and troubles me. I resolve to act boldly, but when I am assailed even by a small temptation, I am in sore straits. From a trifling thing sometimes arises a strong temptation; and when I think I am secure, I am almost overwhelmed by a mere breath.

Consider my lowness and weakness, O Lord, for You

1. 2 Tim. ii, 3.   2. Ps. xxxii, 5.

know all things. Have mercy on me, and raise me from the mire, that I may not stick fast in it,[1] nor remain prostrate. It is this that often defeats and confounds me in Your eyes – that I am so prone to fall and so weak in resisting my passions. And although I do not yield to them entirely, yet their assaults trouble and distress me, so that I am weary of living constantly at conflict. My weakness is apparent to me, for evil fancies rush in on me more readily than they depart.

Most mighty God of Israel, zealous lover of souls, I pray You remember the toil and grief of Your servant, and support him in all his undertakings. Strengthen me with heavenly courage, lest my old and wicked enemy the flesh, not yet wholly subject to the spirit, prevail and gain the upper hand. For against this I must fight while breath remains in this troublous life. Alas, what a life is this, where trials and sorrows never cease, and where all things are full of snares and foes! For when one trial or temptation departs, another takes its place; and even while the conflict rages, other troubles arise, innumerable and unexpected.

How can we love life, when it holds so much bitterness, and is subject to so many sorrows and calamities? How, indeed, can that be called life, which breeds death and pain in such full measure? Yet it is loved, and many find great delight in it. The world is often blamed for its falseness and vanity, but it is not readily abandoned: the desires of the body exercise too strong a hold. Some things cause us to love the world, others to hate it. The desires of the body, the desires of the eyes, and the pride of life[2] all draw us to love the world; but the pains and sorrows that justly ensue cause us to hate and weary of it.

Alas, a perverted pleasure overcomes the mind that surrenders to the world, and counts it a delight to lie among the brambles,[3] for it has neither seen nor tasted the sweetness

1. Ps. xxv, 16; lxix, 14.   2. 1 John ii, 16.   3. Job xxx, 7.

of God and the inner joy of holiness. But they who perfectly despise the world and study to live under God's holy rule know something of that heavenly sweetness promised to all who sincerely forsake the world. They see most clearly how sadly the world goes astray, and how grievously it is deceived.

CHAPTER 21

How we must Rest in God Alone above all Things

THE DISCIPLE. Above all things and in all things rest always in the Lord, O my soul, for He is the everlasting rest of the Saints.

A Prayer

Grant me, most dear and loving Jesus, to rest in You above created things;[1] above health and beauty, above all glory and honour; above all power and dignity, above all knowledge and skill; above all fame and praise, above all sweetness and consolation; above all hope and promise, above all merit and desire; above all gifts and favours that You can bestow and shower upon us; above all joy and jubilation that the mind can conceive and know; above Angels and Archangels and all the hosts of Heaven; above all things visible and invisible; and above everything that is not Yourself, O my God.

O Lord my God, You transcend all things; You alone are most high, most mighty, most sufficient and complete, most sweet and comforting. You alone are most full of beauty and glory, in Whom all good things in their perfection exist, both now and ever have been, and ever will be. All, therefore, is too small and unsatisfying that You can give me

1. Rom. viii, 19.

beside Yourself, or that You can reveal and promise me of Yourself unless I can see and fully possess You. For my heart cannot rest nor be wholly content until it rests in You, rising above all Your gifts and creatures.

O Lord Jesus Christ, spouse of the soul, lover of purity, and Lord of creation, who will give me wings of perfect liberty, that I may fly to You,[1] and be at rest? When shall I be set free, and taste Your sweetness, O Lord my God? When shall I become recollected in You, that for love of You I may no longer be conscious of myself, but of You alone in a manner not known to all men, and above all perception and measure? But now I mourn and bear my unhappy lot with grief, for many evils happen in this vale of sorrows, which often disturb, sadden and darken my path. They often hinder and distract, entice, and entangle me, so that I cannot approach You freely, nor yet enjoy the sweet embrace which You prepare for the souls of the blessed.

O Jesus, Brightness of eternal glory and comfort of the pilgrim soul, hear my cry, and regard my utter desolation. Words fail me in Your presence; let my silence speak for me. How long will my Lord delay His coming? Come to me, Lord, poor and little as I am, and bring me joy. Stretch out Your hand, and deliver me from all my misery and pain. Come, Lord, come, for without You no day or hour is happy; without You my table is without its guest, for You alone are my joy. Sadness is my lot, and I am like a man imprisoned and loaded with chains, until You refresh me with the light of Your presence, and show me Your face as my friend. Let others seek whom they will besides You, but nothing ever can or will give me joy but Yourself alone, my God, my Hope, and my eternal Salvation. I will not keep silent, nor cease from urgent prayer till Your grace returns and my heart leaps at the sound of Your voice.

1. Ps. lv, 6.

CHRIST. See, I am here. I have come at your cry. Your tears and your soul's longing, your humiliation and contrition of heart have moved Me to come to you.

THE DISCIPLE. Lord, I have called You and longed for You. I am ready to renounce everything for Your sake, who first moved me to seek You. Blessed be Your Name, O Lord, for Your goodness to Your servant, according to the richness of Your mercies.[1] What more can Your servant say, Lord? He can only humble himself entirely in Your presence, ever mindful of his own wickedness and unworthiness. For none can compare with You,[2] among all the wonders of heaven and earth. All Your works are good, Your judgements are true,[3] and by Your providence are all things ruled. Praise and glory to You, O Wisdom of the Father! Let my soul, my lips, and all creation join in Your blessing and Your praise!

CHAPTER 22

On Being Mindful of God's Blessings

THE DISCIPLE. Open my heart, O Lord, to know Your law, and teach me to live according to Your commandments.[4] Grant me to know Your will, and reverently to consider all Your countless blessings, that henceforward I may yield You due and worthy thanks. I know and confess that I am wholly unable to render You proper thanks, even for the least of the many blessings that You grant me, for I am less than the least of Your gifts. When I consider Your boundless generosity, my spirit grows faint at its greatness.

Whatever powers of soul and body we possess, outwardly or inwardly, natural or supernatural, are Your own gifts,

1. Ps. cxix, 65; cvi, 45.   3. Ps. xix, 9.
2. Ps. lxxxvi, 8.   4. Ps. cxix, 1; 2 Macc. i, 4.

and proclaim the bounty of the loving and good God, from whom we receive all good gifts. And whether we receive more or less, all gifts are Yours, and without You we have nothing. Thus, whoever has received abundant gifts may not on that account boast of his merits, nor exalt himself above his fellows, nor despise any who are less richly endowed; for the greater and better a man is, the less he attributes to himself, and the more humbly and devoutly he returns thanks to God. He who holds himself in humble esteem, and judges himself most unworthy, is most fitted to receive God's greatest gifts.

One who has received lesser gifts should not on that account be grieved, or envious of those who are more richly endowed than himself. Rather, he should turn to You and praise Your goodness, for Your gifts are given generously, freely, and readily, without respect of persons.[1] All good things come of You; therefore in all things You are to be praised.[2] You alone know what is right for each to receive; and it is not for us to judge why one has less and another more, for You alone can weigh the merits of each.

O Lord God, I count it a great mercy not to possess many of those gifts which outwardly appear praiseworthy and admirable in the eyes of men. For a man who recognizes his own poverty and worthlessness should not be sad and sorry, nor be dejected on that account; rather should he take comfort and be glad, for You, O God, have chosen the poor, the humble, and the despised of this world to be Your own familiar friends[3] and servants. Your Apostles are themselves witnesses of this, whom You have made princes over the whole earth.[4] Yet they lived in this world without complaint, being so humble, simple, and without malice or

1. Rom. ii, 11.   3. John xv, 15; 1 Cor.   4. Ps. xlv, 16.
2. Rom. xi, 36.   i, 27.

deceit, that they were glad to endure reproaches for Your Name's sake;[1] and what the world seeks to avoid, they embraced with ready gladness.

Nothing should give so much joy to one who loves You and receives your blessings, as that Your holy will and the good pleasure of Your eternal purpose should be accomplished in him. With this he should be so greatly comforted and content, that he would as gladly be accounted the least of men as others might desire to be accounted great. He would be as peaceable and content in the last place as in the first;[2] as willing to be a despised outcast of no name or reputation, as to be honoured and exalted among the great. Your will and the honour of Your Name must come before all else; this will bring greater comfort and richer pleasure than all other benefits that have been, or may be given.

CHAPTER 23

On Four Things that Bring Peace

CHRIST. My son, I will now teach you the way of peace and true freedom.

THE DISCIPLE. Lord, instruct me, I pray. I am eager to learn.

CHRIST. My son, resolve to do the will of others rather than your own.[3]

Always choose to possess less rather than more.[4]

Always take the lowest place, and regard yourself as less than others.[5]

Desire and pray always that God's will may be perfectly fulfilled in you.[6]

A man who observes these rules shall come to enjoy peace and tranquillity of soul.

1. Acts v, 41.   3. Matt. xxvi, 39.   5. Luke xiv, 10.
2. Luke xiv, 10.   4. Matt. x, 10.   6. Matt. vi, 10.

THE DISCIPLE. Lord, in these few words of Yours lie the whole secret of perfection. If I could only faithfully observe them, no trouble could distress me. For whenever I am anxious and weary, I find that it is because I have strayed from Your teaching. All things are in Your power, and You always long to bring souls to perfection. Give me your grace ever more richly; help me to keep Your word and advance my salvation.

A Prayer against Evil Thoughts

My Lord and God, do not abandon me; remember my need, for many evil thoughts and horrid fears trouble my mind and terrify my soul. How shall I pass through them unhurt? How shall I break their power over me? You have said, 'I will go before you, and will humble the proud upon earth.[1] I will open the gates of the prison, and reveal to you the hidden treasures and secrets of the ages.' Do, O Lord, as You have said, and let Your coming put to flight all wicked thoughts. It is my hope and comfort that I can turn to You in all my troubles, put my trust in You, call upon You in my heart, and wait Your comfort in patience.

A Prayer for Mental Light

O merciful Jesus, send the brightness of Your light into my mind, and banish all darkness from the sanctuary of my heart. Restrain my many wayward thoughts, and destroy the temptations that beset me with such violence. Let Your great strength be with me in the fight, and overcome the seducing desires of the flesh, that rage in me like evil beasts. By Your power establish peace,[2] and let Your praises be sung in the temple of a pure heart. Command the winds and storm;[3] subdue the fury of the seas and the blast of the

1. Isa. xlv, 2.　　　2. Ps. cxxii, 7.　　　3. Matt. viii, 26.

north wind, and there shall be a great calm. Send out Your light[1] and Your truth to shine over the world; for until Your light illuminates my soul, I am dull earth, formless and empty.[2] Pour forth Your grace from above, and bathe my heart in the dew of Heaven. Supply fresh streams of devotion to water the face of the earth,[3] and produce good and perfect fruit. Inspire my mind, now burdened by my sins, and fix my whole desire on heavenly things, so that, having once tasted the sweetness of eternal joys, I may turn with distaste from all the passing pleasures of this world. Release me, and free my heart from all dependence on the passing consolation of wicked things, since none of these things can yield true satisfaction or appease my longings. Unite me to Yourself by the unbreakable bonds of love. You alone can satisfy the soul that loves You, and without You the world is worthless.

CHAPTER 24
On the Evils of Curiosity

CHRIST. Beware of vain curiosity, My son, and do not busy yourself in profitless matters;[4] what are they to you? Follow me.[5] What concern is it of yours whether a man is good or evil, or what he says and does? You will not be called on to answer for others, but you will certainly have to give a full account of your own life.[6] Why, then, must you meddle where you have no need? I know the hearts of all men, and nothing under the sun is hid from My knowledge. I know the life of every man – his thoughts, his desires and his intentions. Therefore trust yourself entirely to My care, and let your heart be at peace. Let the meddle-

1. Ps. xliii, 3.   3. Gen. ii, 6.   5. John xxi, 22.
2. Gen. i, 2.   4. I Tim. v, 13.   6. Rom. xiv, 12.

some man trouble himself as he will; his words and deeds will recoil on his own head, for he cannot deceive Me.

Do not court the favour of powerful patrons, nor popular favour, not even the particular affection of friends. All these things are distractions, and fill the heart with uncertainty. If you will but await My coming, and throw open the door of your heart, I Myself will speak to you, and reveal to you My secrets. Be ready; watch and pray. Above all, be humble.

CHAPTER 25

On Lasting Peace and True Progress

CHRIST. I have said, 'Peace I leave with you; My own peace I give you. Not as the world gives do I give you.'[1] All men want peace, but all do not seek those things that bring true peace. My peace is with the humble and gentle of heart,[2] and depends on great patience. If you listen to Me, and follow My words, you shall find true peace.

THE DISCIPLE. What must I do, Lord?

CHRIST. Keep guard over your whole life, your actions and words. Direct all your efforts to the single purpose of pleasing Me: seek and desire Myself alone. Never make rash judgements on the behaviour of others, and do not interfere when your opinion is not sought. If you do as I say, you will seldom be troubled in mind. But do not imagine that you can avoid anxiety in this life, or that you may never experience sorrow of heart or pain of body, for true peace is only to be found in the state of eternal rest. So do not think that you have found true peace when you happen to experience no trouble, and do not think that all is well when no one opposes you. Nor should you imagine that everything is perfect when everything happens in

1. John xiv, 27.   2. Matt. xi, 29.

accordance with your wishes. Do not hold an exaggerated opinion of yourself, or believe that you are a favourite of God when you enjoy the grace of great devotion and sweetness; for it is not by these things that the true lover of holiness is known, or is a man's spiritual progress dependent on such things.

THE DISCIPLE. Lord, on what then does it depend?

CHRIST. On complete surrender of your heart to the will of God, not seeking to have your own way either in great matters or small, in time or in eternity. If you will make this surrender, you will thank God with equal gladness both in good times and in bad, and will accept everything, as from His hand, with an untroubled mind. Be courageous and of such unshakeable faith that, when spiritual comfort is withdrawn, you may prepare your heart for even greater trials. Do not think it unjust that you should suffer so much, but confess that I am just in all My dealings, and praise My holy Name. In so doing, you will walk in the true and noble way of peace, and I will surely come to you again and give you great joy.[1] Only think humbly of yourself, and I promise you as great peace[2] as man may enjoy in this life.

CHAPTER 26

On the Excellence of a Free Mind

THE DISCIPLE. Lord, one who desires perfection must make it his first task to keep his mind at all times set on heavenly things. By so doing, he can pass carefree through many troubles, not as one who has not the wit to realize the dangers that beset him, but in the strength of a free mind, unfettered by undue attachment to worldly things.

Most loving God, I beg You so to preserve me that I am

1. Job xxxiii, 26.   2. Ps. lxxii, 7.

not overborne by the cares of this life. Keep me, also, from becoming the servant of my body's many needs, that I may not become absorbed in its pleasures. Save me from all the pitfalls that beset my soul, that they may not overwhelm and crush me. I do not ask to be preserved from those things that vain and worldly men pursue with such ardour, but rather from those miseries that so heavily burden and impede the soul of Your servant, who lies under the curse common to all mortal men.[1] It is these miseries that prevent my soul from entering into the true liberty of the spirit whenever I would. My Lord God, my Delight above all delights, make bitter to me all worldly pleasure that draws me away from the love of eternal joys, and wickedly seduces me by promising me all the joys of the present. Let me not be overcome by flesh and blood,[2] I entreat You. Let not the world and its brief glory deceive me, nor the Devil and his cunning overthrow me. Give me strength to resist, patience to endure, and constancy to persevere. Give me the rich graces of Your spirit rather than all the pleasures of the world and supplant all worldly love by the love of Your Name. A man of fervent spirit grudges much attention to food, drink, clothing and other bodily needs. Grant me to use these things with moderation, and not to be over-concerned about them.[3] It is not right to ignore them, for nature bids us supply their needs; but the law of holiness forbids us to crave for needless luxuries, since the body then revolts against the spirit. In all things, I pray You, let Your hand guide and govern me, that moderation may be my rule at all times.

1. Gen. iii, 17; Rom.   2. Rom. xii, 21; Gal.   3. Matt. vi, 25.
vii, 11.   i, 16.

CHAPTER 27

How Self-Love Hinders our Search for God

CHRIST. My son, you must give all for All, and keep back nothing of yourself from Me. Know that self-love does you more harm than anything else in the world. All things hold your heart a prisoner in greater or less degree, in proportion to the love and regard that you bear them. If your love is pure, simple,[1] and controlled, you will not become the slave of these things. Do not hanker after things that you may not rightly have, and possess nothing that may hinder your spiritual progress, or rob you of inward freedom. It is strange that you are not willing to trust yourself to Me with all your heart, together with all that you may desire or enjoy.

Why exhaust yourself in useless grief? Why burden yourself with needless anxieties? Trust in My goodwill towards you, and you will suffer no hurt. If you want this thing or that, or to be here or there in order to satisfy your convenience and pleasure, you will never be at rest, nor free from care. There will always be something that does not please you, and everywhere you will find someone who opposes your wishes.

Our advantage does not consist in winning or increasing possessions; it lies rather in being indifferent to such things, and eradicating the desire for them from our hearts. These harmful desires include not only love of riches, but also ambition for honours and vain praise. Remember that all these things pass away with the world. It matters little where we live and work, if we lack fervour, nor can any peace be lasting that is sought in external affairs. Unless your life is built on firm foundations, and unless you stand firm in My strength, you will hardly be able to amend your life. So

1. Matt. vi, 22.

when opportunity for self-surrender arises, seize it. You will discover the secret in what you had hitherto tried to avoid; indeed, you will find even more.

A Prayer for a Pure Heart and Heavenly Wisdom

Strengthen me, O Lord God, by the grace of Your Holy Spirit.[1] Grant me inward power and strength,[2] and empty my heart of all profitless anxiety and care.[3] Let me never be drawn away from You by desire for anything else, whether noble or base, but help me to realize that all things are passing, and myself with them. Nothing in this world is lasting, and everything in this life is uncertain, troubling to the spirit.[4] How wise is the man who knows these truths! Grant me heavenly wisdom, O Lord, that above all else I may learn to search for and discover You; to know and love You; and to see all things as they really are, and as You in Your wisdom have ordered them. May I prudently avoid those who flatter me, and deal patiently with those who oppose me. True wisdom cannot be swayed by every wordy argument,[5] and pays no regard to the cunning flatteries of evil men. Only thus shall we go forward steadily on the road on which we have set out.

CHAPTER 28
Against Slander

CHRIST. My son, do not take it to heart if others think ill of you, and say unpleasant things about you. Consider yourself to be even worse than they imagine, and regard yourself as the weakest of men. If your inner life is strong, you will not pay much heed to passing words. A wise man remains

1. Ps. li, 12.　　　3. Matt. vi, 34.　　　5. Eph. iv, 14.
2. Eph. iii, 16.　　　4. Eccles. i, 14; ii, 11.

silent when beset by evil; he turns to Me in his heart, and is untroubled by man's judgements.

Do not let your peace depend on what people say of you, for whether they speak good or ill of you makes no difference to what you are. True peace and joy is to be found in Me alone. He who is neither anxious to please nor afraid to displease men enjoys true peace. All unrest of heart and distraction of mind spring from disorderly affections and groundless fears.

CHAPTER 29

How we should Bless God in all Trouble

THE DISCIPLE. Blessed be Your holy Name for ever, O Lord.[1] I know that it is by Your will that temptation and trouble come upon me. I cannot escape it, but must needs come to You for help, that it may be turned to my good. Lord, I am tormented and uneasy in mind, and my present troubles weigh heavy on me. Most loving Father, what may I say? I am in dire straits. Save me from this hour.[2] Yet it is for Your glory that I have been brought to this hour, and that I may learn that You alone can deliver me from the depths of my humiliation. Of Your goodness, deliver me, O Lord.[3] For what can I do, helpless as I am; and where can I go without Your aid? Give me patience, Lord, even in this trial. Grant me help, and I shall fear nothing, however hard pressed I may be.

And now, in this trouble, this shall be my prayer, 'Your will be done.'[4] I have fully deserved this trouble, and must bear it. Let me bear it patiently, until the storm is past and better days return. I know that Your almighty power can

1. 1 Peter i, 3.   3. Ps. xxxvii, 40.
2. John xii, 27.   4. Matt. vi, 10.

remove even this trial from me and lessen its violence, so that I am not completely crushed by it. Often in times past, my God and my Mercy, You have done this for me. And the harder it is for me, the easier it is for You to change my way,[1] O God most high.

CHAPTER 30

On Asking God's Help, and the Certainty of his Grace

CHRIST. My son, I am the Lord, who give strength in time of trouble.[2] Come to Me when the struggle goes hard with you.[3] Your slowness in turning to prayer is the greatest obstacle to receiving My heavenly comfort. For, when you should earnestly seek Me, you first turn to many other comforts, and hope to restore yourself by worldly means. It is only when all these things have failed that you remember that I am the Saviour of all who put their trust in Me;[4] and that, apart from Me, there can be no effective help, no sound counsel, and no lasting remedy. But now, with spirit renewed after the tempest, gather fresh strength and light in My mercies.[5] For I am near, and will restore all things, not only completely, but generously and in full measure.

Is anything too hard for Me?[6] Shall I be like one who does not fulfil his promise? Where is your faith? Stand firm, and persevere. Be courageous and patient, and help will come to you in due time. Wait patiently for Me, and I Myself will come and heal you. Temptation is your testing – there is no cause for alarm or fear. Sorrow upon sorrow can be the only result if you worry about the future. Sufficient to the day is the evil in it.[7] It is quite vain and useless to be either

1. Ps. lxxvii, 10.   4. Ps. xvii, 7.   6. Jer. xxxii, 27.
2. Nahum i, 7.   5. Ecclus. xxxv, 20.   7. Matt. vi, 34.
3. Matt. xi, 28.

133

anxious or pleased about the future, for what you anticipate may never happen.

The mind of man is prone to delusions, but to be deceived by the suggestions of the Devil is a sign of spiritual weakness. Satan does not care whether it be by truth or falsehood that he mocks and deceives you; or whether he obtains your downfall through love of the present or fear of the future. Therefore, let not your heart be troubled, neither let it be afraid.[1] Trust in Me, and put your whole confidence in My mercy.[2] When you think I am far away, then often I am nearest to you. And when you think the battle almost lost, then the reward of all your toil is often near. All is not lost when anything turns out contrary to your plans. Therefore do not allow your feelings of the moment to obscure your judgement, nor yield to depression as though all hope of recovery were lost.

Do not imagine yourself utterly forsaken if for a while I have allowed some trial to harass you, or withdrawn the comfort that you desire; for this is the way to the Kingdom of Heaven. Be assured that it is better for you, and for all My servants, to struggle against difficulties than to have everything as you wish. I know your secret thoughts, and it is necessary for your salvation that you should sometimes be deprived of spiritual joys, lest you become conceited in your happy state, and complacently imagine yourself better than you are. What I have granted, I can take away, and restore it when I choose.

When I grant comfort, it remains Mine; and when I withdraw it, I am not taking anything that is yours, for every good gift and every perfect gift is Mine alone.[3] If I send you trouble and affliction, do not be indignant or downhearted; for I can swiftly help you, and turn all your

1. John xiv, 27.   2. Ps. xci, 2.   3. James i, 17.

sorrow into joy. Notwithstanding, I keep My own counsel, and in all My dealings with you, give Me due praise.

If you are wise and have right judgement, you will never despair or be discouraged. On the contrary, if I scourge you with trouble and do not spare you,[1] be glad and grateful, and regard it as cause for joy. For, 'as My Father has loved Me, so do I love you,'[2] were My words to my well loved disciples, whom I did not send out to enjoy the pleasures of the world, but to fight hard battles; not to win honours, but contempt; not to be idle, but industrious; not to rest, but to bring forth much fruit with patience.[3]

CHAPTER 31
On Forsaking Creatures to Find the Creator

THE DISCIPLE. Lord, I am greatly in need of yet more abundant grace if I am to reach that state where no creature can impede my progress. For as long as anything holds me back, I cannot come freely to You. One who desired to fly freely to You said, 'Who will give me wings like a dove? I will fly, and be at rest.'[4] And who is more perfectly at rest than the man of single purpose?[5] Who more free than he who desires nothing upon earth? Rapt in spirit, a man must rise above all created things, and perfectly forsaking himself, see clearly that nothing in creation can compare with the Creator. But unless a man is freed from dependence on creatures, he cannot turn freely to the things of God. This is the reason why there are so few contemplatives, for there are few who can free themselves entirely from transitory things.

A soul needs much grace to be raised up and carried

1. Job vi, 10.   3. Luke viii, 15.   5. Matt. vi, 22.
2. John xv, 9.   4. Ps. lv, 6.

beyond itself. Yet, unless a man's soul is raised, set free from all attachment to earthly things, and wholly united to God, neither his knowledge nor his possessions are of any value. So long as he esteems as precious anything outside the One, Infinite, and Eternal Good, he will remain mean and earth-bound in spirit. For whatever is not God is nothing, and is to be accounted nothing. There is a great difference between the wisdom of a devout man enlightened by God, and the knowledge of a learned and studious scholar. More noble by far is the learning infused from above by divine grace, than that painfully acquired by the industry of man.

Many desire the grace of contemplation, but few take the trouble to practise what is essential to it. It is a great obstacle if we rely on external signs and the experience of the senses, and pay small regard to the perfecting of self-discipline. I hardly know what motives can inspire us, or what our purpose may be, when we who wish to be considered spiritual take so much trouble and are so concerned with trivial, daily affairs, and so seldom give our full and earnest attention to our interior life.

Alas, after a short meditation we break off, and do not make a strict examination of our lives. We do not consider where our affections really lie, nor are we grieved at the sinfulness of our whole life. Yet it was because of the wickedness of men that the Flood came upon the earth.[1] When our inner inclinations are corrupted, the actions that spring from them are also corrupted. And this is a sign of our lack of inner strength; for from a pure heart alone springs the fruit of a holy life.

A man's achievements are often discussed, but seldom the principles by which he lives. We inquire whether he is brave, handsome, rich, clever, a good writer, a fine singer, or a hard worker: but whether he is humble-minded,

1. Gen. vi, 12.

patient and gentle, devout and spiritual is seldom mentioned. Nature regards the outward characteristics of a man: Grace considers his inner disposition. And while Nature is often misled, Grace trusts in God and cannot be deceived.

CHAPTER 32
On Self-Denial, and Renunciation of our Desires

CHRIST. My son, complete self-denial is the only road to perfect liberty. Those who are obsessed by self-interest and self-love are slaves of their own desires;[1] they are greedy, inquisitive, and discontented. They spend themselves in pleasures, but never in the service of Jesus Christ, their whole interest being in passing affairs. But all that is not of God shall perish utterly. Observe this simple counsel of perfection: Forsake all, and you shall find all. Renounce desire, and you shall find peace. Give this due thought, and when you have put it into practice, you will understand all things.

THE DISCIPLE. Lord, this is not the work of a single day, and no easy matter. These few words contain the whole way of spiritual perfection.

CHRIST. My son, do not be discouraged or diverted from your purpose at hearing of this way of perfection. Rather let it spur you to higher things, and, at least, to set your heart on them. If only you would do this, and attain that state where you cease to be a lover of self, and stand ready to do My will and His whom I have appointed as your Father, you would greatly please Me, and your whole life would be filled with joy and peace. Your have still many things to renounce, and unless you surrender them to Me without reserve, you cannot obtain what you ask of Me. I counsel you to buy

1. 2 Tim. iii, 2.

from Me gold, refined in the fire, that you may be rich[1] in that heavenly wisdom that rejects all worthless things. Despise the wisdom of the world, and every temptation to please others or yourself.

I have said, exchange what men consider desirable and honourable for that which they hold in low esteem. For true heavenly wisdom, having no exalted opinion of itself,[2] seeks no recognition from the world, is almost disregarded by men, and seems to them useless and of no importance. Many pay it lip-service, but it plays no part in their lives. Yet this is the precious pearl, that remains hidden from many.[3]

CHAPTER 33
On Inconstancy of Heart

CHRIST. My son, do not trust your affections, for they are changeable and inconstant. All your life you are subject to change, even against your inclination.[4] At one time you are cheerful, at another sad; now peaceful, now troubled; now full of devotion, now wholly lacking it; now zealous, now slothful; now grave, now gay. But the wise man, who is well versed in spiritual matters, stands above these changing emotions. He pays small regard to his momentary feelings and whims, but directs all the powers of his mind towards the right and true end. Thus, having fixed his gaze and kept his intention constantly on Me, he can remain single in purpose, and unshaken under all circumstances.

The more single his purpose,[5] the more steadily will a man pass through all the storms of life. But in many, this single purpose becomes obscured; for men pay ready atten-

1. Rev. iii, 18.   3. Matt. xiii, 46.   5. Matt. vi, 22.
2. Rom. xii, 16.   4. Rom. viii, 20.

tion to any pleasant thing that comes their way, and it is a rare thing to find anyone wholly free from the sin of self-interest. Thus the Jews once came out to Bethany to Martha and Mary, not for Jesus' sake only, but to see Lazarus.[1] Therefore make your intention pure, single, and upright, that it may be directed to Me alone without hindrance.

CHAPTER 34

On God's Graciousness to Those who Love Him

THE DISCIPLE. Oh, my God and my All![2] What more can I possess?

What greater joy can I desire? Word of sweetness and delight to all who love the Word better than the world and its treasures! My God and my All! To the wise, these words suffice, and he who loves You will delight to repeat them again and again. When You are present, all is joy; when You are absent, all is gloom. You bring rest to the heart, true peace, and true gladness. You cause us to think well of all, and to praise you in all, for nothing can give us lasting joy without You.

Whoever knows Your joys will find joy in all things; but whoever knows nothing of Your joys will find no joy in anything. Those who are worldly-wise and sensual-minded lack Your wisdom, for in the world lurks much vanity, and in the flesh, death.[3] Those who follow You by despising worldly things and mortifying their bodily desires are truly wise; they abandon illusion for truth, they forsake the flesh for the spirit. These have their delight in God alone, and whatever good they discover in creatures they ascribe wholly to the glory of their Maker. But how vast is the difference

1. John xii, 9.   3. Rom. viii, 5.
2. 1 Cor. xv, 28; John xx, 28.

between enjoyment of the Creator and enjoyment of His creation; between things of Eternity and those of time; between Light Uncreated and light created!

A Prayer for Light

O Light everlasting, surpassing all created light![1] Pour forth from Heaven the glorious rays of Your light, and pierce the very depths of my heart! Purify, gladden, light, and quicken the powers of my spirit, that it may hold to You with joy unspeakable. Oh, when shall come that blessed and longed for hour, when You fill me with Your presence, and be to me All in all.[2] Until You grant this, I can know no fullness of joy. As yet, alas, my lower nature is strong within me; it is not yet wholly crucified, nor entirely dead.[3] It still fights strongly against the spirit, stirring up conflicts within me, and will not allow the kingdom of the soul to remain at peace. O Christ, who rules the power of the sea and quells its raging waves,[4] come near and help me! Scatter the nations that delight in war,[5] and overcome them in Your strength.[6] Display Your mighty power, I pray, and show Yourself glorious in might; I have no hope nor refuge[7] but in You, O Lord my God.

CHAPTER 35

How There is no Security from Temptation

CHRIST. My son, there is no security from temptation in this life, and as long as you live, you will need spiritual weapons. Your road lies among enemies, and you are liable to attack from every quarter. Unless you carry the shield of patience,[8]

1. Ps. xxvii, 1; John viii, 12.	3. Rom. vi, 6.	6. Ps. lx, 12.
	4. Ps. lxxxix, 9.	7. Ps. xxxi, 2.
2. 1 Cor. xv, 28.	5. Ps. lxviii, 30.	8. Eph. vi, 11.

you will not long remain unwounded. And, unless you fix your heart on Me, with a firm resolve to suffer gladly for My sake, you will not endure the heat of battle, nor win the crown of the Saints. Bear all things manfully, and strike lustily at your enemies, for the Bread of Heaven is the reward of the victor,[1] and the slothful is left in unutterable wretchedness.

If you look for rest in this life, how can you attain eternal rest? Dispose yourself not to rest, but to patient endurance. Seek true peace not on earth, but in Heaven; not in man, nor in any other creature, but in God alone. For love of God, cheerfully endure everything – labour, sorrow, temptation, provocation, anxiety, necessity, weakness, injury and insult; censure, humiliation, disgrace, contradiction and contempt. All these things foster your growth in virtue, for they test the unproved servant of Christ, and form the jewels of his heavenly crown. I will grant an eternal reward for your brief toil, and boundless glory for your passing trouble.

Do you imagine that you can always have spiritual joys at will? My Saints did not, but had many troubles, countless trials, and great desolation of soul. But they patiently endured all these things, and trusted in God rather than themselves, knowing that 'the sufferings of this present time are not worthy to be compared with the glory to be won hereafter.'[2] Do you wish to enjoy immediately what many others have only won after much sorrow and struggle? Wait for the Lord; fight manfully and with high courage.[3] Do not despair, do not desert your post, but steadfastly devote yourself body and soul to the glory of God. I will give you a rich reward,[4] and will be with you in all your troubles.[5]

1. Rev. ii, 17.   3. Ps. xxvii, 14.   5. Ps. xci, 15.
2. Rom. viii, 18.   4. Matt. xvi, 27.

Against the Vain Judgements of Men

CHRIST. My son, trust in God with all your heart. If your conscience bears witness to your devotion and innocence, you need not fear the judgements of men. It is a good and holy thing to suffer in this way, and it will not be a burden to the humble heart that trusts in God rather than itself. Many people talk too much, and little attention should be paid them. Moreover, it is quite impossible to please everyone. Although Saint Paul endeavoured to be pleasing to all men in the Lord,[1] and became all things to all men, yet he cared very little what they thought of himself.[2] He did whatever lay in his power to bring instruction and salvation to others, but even he could not escape being misjudged and despised by others. Accordingly he trusted himself wholly to God, who knows all things, and opposed the shield of patience and humility to the unjust accusations, empty lies and vain boasts of his detractors. Notwithstanding, sometimes he replied to them, lest his silence should give scandal to the weak.[3]

Why should you fear mortal man?[4] Today he is here; tomorrow he is gone for ever. Fear God, and you need never fear man. What real harm can the words or actions of any man do you? He injures himself rather than you, and he cannot escape the judgement of God, whoever he be. Keep God always before you, and do not engage in bitter controversies. Even if for the present you seem to suffer defeat and undeserved disgrace, do not complain nor lessen your due reward through impatience.[5] Instead, raise your eyes to Me in Heaven, for I have power to deliver you from

1. I Cor. ix, 22.
2. I Cor. iv, 3.
3. Acts xxvi, 1; Phil. i, 14.
4. Isa. li, 12.
5. Heb. xii, 1.

all shame and wrong, and to reward every man according to his merits.[1]

CHAPTER 37
How Surrender of Self Brings Freedom of Heart

CHRIST. My son, renounce self, and you shall find me.[2] Retain no private choice or personal interest, and you will always be the gainer. As soon as you yield yourself unreservedly into My hands, I will grant you even richer graces.

THE DISCIPLE. How often shall I yield myself, and in what way forsake myself, Lord?

CHRIST. Always, and at all times, in small things as well as in great. I make no exceptions, for I desire to have you wholly divested of self: otherwise, unless you are wholly stripped of self-will, how can you be Mine, or I yours? The sooner you do this, the better it will be with you, and the more completely and sincerely you do it, the better you will please Me, and the greater will be your gain.

Some resign themselves, but with some reservation; these do not put their whole trust in God, and are therefore concerned to provide for themselves. Others at first offer everything, but later are overcome by temptation, and return to their former state. These make very little progress in virtue, and will never obtain the true freedom of heart, nor enjoy the favour of My friendship,[3] unless they first make a complete surrender and daily offering of themselves to Me. Without this, no fruitful union with Me can exist or endure.

I have often said to you, and I now say once more: Renounce yourself, surrender yourself, and you shall enjoy

1. Rom. ii, 6.　2. Matt. xvi, 24.　3. Exod. xxxiii, 11; John xv, 14, 15.

great inner peace. Give all for all, look for nothing, ask nothing in return: rest purely and trustingly in Me, and you shall possess Me. Then you will be free in heart, and no darkness will oppress your soul. Strive for this, pray for this, desire this one thing – that you may be stripped clean of all selfishness, and follow Jesus in complete self-abandonment, dying to self that you may live to Me for ever. Then will all vain fantasies be put to flight, and all evil disorders and groundless fears vanish. Then will all fear and dread depart, and all disordered love die in you.

CHAPTER 38
On the Right Ordering of our Affairs

CHRIST. My son, take great care to ensure that in every place, action, and outward occupation you remain inwardly free and your own master. Control circumstances, and do not allow them to control you. Only so can you be master and ruler of your actions, not their servant or slave; a free man and a true Christian, enjoying the freedom and high destiny of the children of God.[1] These stand above the things of time, and view those of eternity, seeing in their true light both earthly and heavenly things. The things of this world have no hold over the children of God; on the contrary, they draw them into their service, and employ them in the ways ordained by God and established by the Heavenly Architect, who has left nothing in His creation without its due place.

Stand firm in all circumstances. Do not judge by outward appearances or reports as men do, but in each instance enter like Moses into the Tabernacle,[2] to ask guidance of the Lord. Sometimes you will receive God's answer, and return instructed on many matters, both present and future. For

1. Rom. viii, 21.   2. Exod. xxxiii, 8.

Moses always had recourse to the Tabernacle to obtain an answer to his doubts and questions, and he took refuge in prayer to support him amidst the dangers and wickednesses of men. Similarly must you take refuge in the depths of your heart, and pray most earnestly for God's help. We read that Joshua and the children of Israel were deceived by the men of Gibeon[1] because they had not first asked counsel of God. Therefore, in giving credit to their statements, they were misled by their pretended piety.

CHAPTER 39
How we should not be Over Anxious

CHRIST. My son, always commit your cause to Me, and I will bring it to a good issue in due time. Wait until I order it, and you will find it to your advantage.

THE DISCIPLE. Lord, I readily commit everything into your hands, for my own judgement is of small value. I wish I were less concerned about the future, and could unreservedly submit myself to Your good pleasure.

CHRIST. My son, a man often labours incessantly to obtain his desire; but when he has obtained it, he begins to change his mind. For man's affections do not remain constant, but tend to move from one object to another. It is therefore no small advantage, if a man can renounce self even in small things. Man's true spiritual progress depends on the denial of self, and he who renounces self is completely free and secure. But the Old Enemy,[2] the Adversary of all good, never ceases to tempt man. Day and night he lies in ambush, hoping to trap the unwary into the snares of his deceit. 'Watch and pray lest you enter into temptation.'[3]

1. Joshua ix, 22.   2. 1 Pet. v, 8.   3. Matt. xxvi, 41.

CHAPTER 40

How Man has no Personal Goodness of which to Boast

THE DISCIPLE. 'Lord, what is man that You are mindful of him, or the son of man, that You visit him.'[1] What has man done to deserve Your grace? Lord, I have no cause to complain if You abandon me; and if Your Will is contrary to my desires, I have no right to plead against it. But this I may rightly think and say, 'Lord, I am nothing and I can do nothing. I have no good of Myself, but am imperfect in every respect, and always tend to nothing. Unless You guide my soul and grant me strength, I become weak and completely helpless.'

You, O Lord, remain ever Yourself,[2] abiding in eternity, good, just, and holy, ordering all things in goodness, justice, and holiness, and disposing them in wisdom. But I, who am always more ready to slip back than go forward, never remain the same, for seven times have passed over me.[3] Yet, when You deign to stretch out Your hand to help me, my state is quickly changed for the better; for You alone, and without human aid, can help and strengthen me, so that I may no longer be unstable, but turn my heart to You alone, and be at peace. No mortal man can comfort me, and if only I could wholly renounce all human comfort – whether to increase my devotion, or because my needs compel me to seek You – then I could rightly trust entirely to Your grace, and rejoice in the gift of Your renewed comfort.

Whenever things go well with me, I offer thanks to You, from whom all proceeds. Before You, I am empty nothingness, a weak and unstable man. I have nothing of which to boast, nothing for which I merit any consideration. Can nothing boast of its nothingness? This would be the height of vanity! Empty conceit is like an evil disease, and the most

1. Ps. viii, 4.   2. Ps. cii, 27.   3. Dan. iv, 16.

monstrous of vanities, for it leads a man away from true glory, and robs him of heavenly grace. For so long as a man is filled with complacency, he displeases You; and while he hankers after popularity and praise, he is deprived of true virtue. True glory and holy joy are to be found in giving glory not to self, but to You; rejoicing not in one's own strength, but in Your Name; taking no pleasure in creatures, unless it be for Your sake. Praised be Your holy Name, not mine. I will praise your Name, but not my own; I will esteem Your doings, not my own: I will bless Your holy Name. I desire no share in the praises of men. You alone are my glory. You alone are the joy of my heart. I will offer You praise and glory every hour of the day; but for myself, I will glory in nothing, unless it be in my own weakness.[1] Let the Jews seek such glory as men give to one another;[2] I will seek the glory that God alone can give. For all human glory, all this world's honours, all earthly titles, compared with Your eternal glory, are mere vanity and foolishness. O blessed Trinity, my God, my Truth, my Mercy, to You alone let all things ascribe all praise, honour, power, and glory throughout endless ages.[3]

CHAPTER 41

On Contempt for Worldly Honours

CHRIST. My son, do not be discouraged if you see others given honours and advancement, while you are overlooked and humiliated. Lift up your heart to Me in Heaven, and the contempt of men will not trouble you.

THE DISCIPLE. Lord, we are blind, and are easily deceived through vanity. If I carefully examine my life, I find that no creature has ever done me wrong, and I have no right to

1. 2 Cor. xii, 5.   2. John v, 44.   3. 1 Tim. i, 17.

complain. But because I have so often and grievously sinned against You, every creature is rightly in arms against me. Shame and contempt are my just due; but to You, O Lord, be praise, honour, and glory. Unless I am ready, willing, and glad to be despised and abandoned by all creatures, and to be regarded as of no consequence, I cannot obtain inward peace and stability, nor can I become spiritually enlightened and fully united to You.

CHAPTER 42

That our Peace cannot Depend on Man

CHRIST. My son, if your peace depends on anyone, by reason of your affection or friendship with him, you will always be unsettled, and dependent on him. But if you turn to the living and eternal Truth, the departure or death of your friend will not distress you. Your love for a friend must rest in Me, and those who are dear to you in this life must be loved only for My sake. No good and lasting friendship can exist without Me, and unless I bless and unite all love it cannot be pure and true. You should be so mortified in your affection towards loved ones that, for your part, you would forego all human companionship. Man draws the nearer to God as he withdraws further from the consolations of this world. And the deeper he descends into himself and the lower he regards himself, the higher he ascends towards God.

He who attributes any goodness to himself, obstructs the coming of God's grace, for the grace of the Holy Spirit always seeks a humble heart. If you would perfectly overcome self and set yourself free from love of creatures, I would come to you with all My grace.[1] But while your

1. I Pet. v, 5.

interest is in creatures, the vision of the Creator is hidden from you. Learn, then, for love of the Creator, to overcome self in everything, and you shall come to the knowledge of God. But so long as anything, however small, occupies too much of your love and regard, it injures the soul and holds you back from attaining the highest Good.

CHAPTER 43

A Warning against Vain and Worldly Learning

CHRIST. My son, do not allow fair phrases and subtle sayings to beguile you; for the Kingdom of God comes not by words, but by My power.[1] Pay attention to My words, for they fire the heart and lighten the understanding, foster contrition and bring all comfort. Never study in order to appear more wise and learned; study rather to overcome your besetting sins, for this will profit you more than will the grasp of intricate problems.

When you have read and mastered many subjects, always return to this fundamental truth: that I am He who teaches man knowledge,[2] and who grants My children a clearer understanding than man can impart. He whom I teach will swiftly gain wisdom and advance far in the life of the spirit. But those who seek curious knowledge from men, and care nothing for My service, will discover only sorrow. In due time Christ will come, the Teacher of teachers and Lord of Angels.[3] He will hear the lessons of all; that is, He will examine each man's conscience. He will search Jerusalem with lamps; the hidden things of darkness will be brought to light,[4] and the tongues of controversy silenced.

I am God, who enable the humble-minded to understand

1. 1 Cor. iv, 20.   3. Col. iii, 4.
2. Ps. xciv, 10; cxix, 130.   4. 1 Cor. iv, 5.

more of the ways of the everlasting Truth in a single moment than ten years of study in the Schools. I teach in silence, without the clamour of controversy, without ambition for honours, without confusion of argument. I teach men to despise earthly things, to find this present life burdensome, to seek eternal things, to shun honours, to endure injuries, to place all trust in Me, to desire nothing but Myself, and to love Me ardently above all things.

There was once a man who loved Me very dearly, who learned My divine secrets, and spoke eloquently of Me. He profited more by renouncing everything than by studying subtleties. For to some I speak on everyday affairs; to others on particular matters; to some I graciously reveal Myself in signs and symbols, while to those who are enlightened I reveal My mysteries.

A book has but a single voice, but is not equally profitable to all who read it. I alone am the Teacher of truth, the Searcher of man's heart, the Discerner of his doings, and I give to each man as I judge right.[1]

CHAPTER 44
On Avoiding Distractions

CHRIST. My son, you must needs be ignorant of many things: so consider yourself as dead, and crucified to the whole world.[2] Furthermore, you must turn a deaf ear to many things, and consider only such as bring peace. It is better to turn away from controversial matters, and leave everyone to hold their own opinions, than to belabour them with quarrelsome arguments. So long as you remain in God's grace, and carry His Will in your heart, you will more easily endure apparent discomfiture.

1. 1 Cor. xii, 11.   2. Col. iii, 3; Gal. vi, 14.

THE DISCIPLE. Lord, to what a pass have we come? We grieve over a worldly loss; we labour and hustle to gain some small profit, forgetting the harm to our souls, and seldom recalling it. We attend to matters of little or no value, and neglect those of the greatest importance. For when a man devotes all his energies to material affairs, he rapidly becomes immersed in them, unless he quickly recovers his senses.

CHAPTER 45

How we should not Believe all we Hear

THE DISCIPLE. Lord, help me in my trouble, for vain is the help of man.[1] How often have I found no loyalty where I expected to find it! And how often have I found it where I least expected! It is useless to place our hope in man; salvation is to be found in You alone, O God.[2] In all that befalls us, we bless You, O Lord our God.

We are weak and unstable, changeable and easily deceived. None of us can guard himself so carefully and completely that he is never deceived nor in doubt. But whoever trusts in You, Lord, and seeks You with a pure heart, does not easily fall. And if he encounters any trouble, however great it be, You will swiftly deliver or comfort him; for You never abandon those who trust in You to the end. Rare indeed is a faithful friend, who stands by his friend in all trouble. And You, Lord, are the most faithful of all friends, and there is none like You.

How wise was the holy soul (Saint Agatha) who said, 'My mind is firmly established and grounded in Christ.' Were this true of myself, I should never fear any man, and no bitter words could disturb me. We cannot foresee the future or provide against evils to come; and if things that we expect

1. Ps. lx, 11.   2. Ps. xxxvii, 39.

often harm us, how can unexpected events do otherwise than seriously harm us? Why have I not made better provision for my unfortunate self, and why have I trusted so readily in others? For we are but mortal men, and nothing if not weak, even if many people imagine and say that we are angels. There is none in whom I can trust, Lord, save Yourself, who are the Truth, and who neither deceives nor can be deceived. But every man is deceitful,[1] weak, unstable and fallible, especially in what he says, so that we should not at once believe even what at first appears to be true.

Your wisdom warns us to beware of man,[2] since a man's enemies are those of his own household,[3] and we may not believe any who says, 'He is here', or 'He is there'.[4] I have learned this to my cost, and I only hope that it may make me more careful and correct my foolishness. 'Be discreet,' says one: 'Be discreet, and keep what I tell you to yourself.' And while I remain silent about it, imagining it to be a secret, he cannot himself keep the silence which he enjoined on me, but at once betrays both himself and me, and goes on his way. From such tales and from such indiscreet folk, protect me, O Lord! Do not let me fall into their power, nor behave in the same way myself. Make my conversation truthful and trustworthy, far removed from slyness. For what I do not tolerate in others, I must myself avoid at all costs.

To remain silent about others makes for peace and goodwill, neither believing all that is said, nor repeating what one has heard. There are few to whom we should open our hearts, but we should always seek You, who see into all hearts. We may not allow ourselves to be carried to and fro by the windy blast of words, but rather pray that all our

1. Rom. iii, 4.   3. Micah vii, 5.
2. Matt. x, 17.   4. Matt. xxiv, 23.

life, both public and private, may be ordered in conformity to Your Will.

A sure way of retaining the grace of heaven is to disregard outward appearances, and diligently to cultivate such things as foster amendment of life and fervour of soul, rather than to cultivate those qualities that seem most popular.

Very many people have been harmed by publicity and by lightly-bestowed praise of their virtues. But grace is most powerful when preserved in silence in this transitory life, which consists wholly of temptation and warfare.

CHAPTER 46

On Putting our Entire Trust in God

CHRIST. My son, stand firm, and trust in Me. What are words, but words only? They fly to and fro, but hurt not so much as a stone. If you are guilty, consider how you should willingly amend; if you have nothing on your conscience, resolve to endure this willingly for God's sake. It is a small thing to endure hard words from time to time, if you are not yet able to bear hard blows. The reason why you take such trifles to heart is that you are still worldly, and pay greater regard to men's opinions than you ought. Because you fear their contempt, you do not like to be corrected for your faults, and you take refuge in excuses.

If you examine yourself more carefully, you will find your heart still full of worldly desires and a foolish anxiety to please men. For when you shrink from the humiliation and reproof that your faults deserve, it is clear that you are not truly humble, neither are you dead to the world, nor the world crucified to you.[1] Listen only to My words, and you will care nothing for ten thousand words of men. Even

1. Gal. vi, 14.

if you were charged with every crime that could be maliciously invented, how could it harm you if you let it pass, and paid absolutely no attention to it? Could such a torrent of words harm a single hair of your head?[1]

But the man who keeps no guard over his heart, and does not regard God, is easily unsettled by a word of reproof; whereas he who trusts in Me and does not cling to his own judgement will fear no man. For I am the Judge and discerner of secrets; I understand the motives of every action; I know both him who inflicts the wrong and him who suffers it. It is by My will and permission that events happen, in order that the thoughts of many hearts may be revealed.[2] I will judge the guilty and the innocent, but firstly I wish to test them in secret judgement.

The witness of men is often false, but My judgement is true: it shall stand, and shall not be set aside. It is hidden from many, and revealed in its fullness only to few. Nevertheless, even though it may appear unjust to the foolish, it does not and cannot err. Therefore, always come to Me for justice, and put no trust in personal opinions.

The just man will not be anxious, whatever God allows to happen to him.[3] Even if a groundless accusation is laid against him, he will not greatly care. Nor will he be unduly elated if he is fairly acquitted by others, for he knows very well that it is I who examine both the heart and the senses, and do not judge according to outward appearances.[4] For those things which men regard as commendable are often blameworthy in My sight.

THE DISCIPLE. O Lord God, most just Judge, strong and patient, who know the weakness and wickedness of man, be my strength and all my trust, for my own conscience is not sufficient. You know what is unknown to me, and I

1. Luke xxi, 18; Acts   2. Luke ii, 35.   4. John vii, 24.
   xxvii, 34.   3. Prov. xii, 21.

should therefore have been humble when blamed, and borne it meekly. Be gracious, and pardon the occasions when I have not done this, and once again give me grace to endure more patiently. Your abundant mercy will better obtain my pardon, than will my fancied innocence satisfy my inmost conscience. For although I may not be conscious of any fault, yet this does not absolve me.[1] If You withhold mercy, no man living can be absolved.[2]

CHAPTER 47
How Burdens must be Borne to win Eternal Life

CHRIST. My son, do not let the work that you have undertaken for My sake break your spirit, nor any hardships discourage you. Let My promise be always your strength and comfort; I can give you a boundless reward. You will not labour here for long, nor will sorrow always be your lot. Wait but a short while, and you will see a speedy end to your troubles. The time will come when all toil and trouble will cease: everything temporal is short lived and of little consequence.

Labour with all your might; work faithfully in My vineyard;[3] I Myself will be Your reward.[4] Write, study, worship, be penitent, keep silence, and pray. Meet all your troubles like a man: eternal life is worth all this and yet greater conflicts. Peace will come at a time known only to the Lord; it will not be day or night as we know it,[5] but everlasting light, boundless glory, abiding peace, and sure rest. You will not say then, 'Who will free me from this mortal body?';[6] nor cry, 'Alas, how long is my exile!',[7] for the

1. 1 Cor. iv, 4.   4. Gen. xv, 1.   6. Rom. vii, 24.
2. Ps. cxliii, 2.   5. Rev. xxii, 5.   7. Ps. cxx, 5.
3. Matt. xx, 7.

power of death will be utterly broken,[1] and full salvation assured. No anxiety will remain, but only blessed joy in the fair and lovely fellowship of the Saints.

If you could but see the Saints crowned in endless glory,[2] you would at once humble yourself to the dust, and would rather be the servant of all than lord it over a single person; for the Saints are now as high exalted as they were formerly accounted by this world low, despicable, and unfit to live. You would not hanker after a pleasant time in this life, but rather be glad to suffer for God's sake, and account it the greatest gain to be considered of small importance among men. If the things of God were your true delight and pierced your inmost heart, you would never complain. Is not all labour to be endured for the sake of eternal life? It is no small matter to win or lose the Kingdom of God. Raise your eyes to Heaven. See, here am I, and with Me are all My Saints, who in this world fought a great fight.[3] They are now filled with joy and consolation; they are now safe and at rest;[4] and they shall remain with Me for ever in the Kingdom of My Father.[5]

CHAPTER 48
On Eternity, and the Limitations of This Life

THE DISCIPLE. O ever-blessed palaces of the heavenly City![6] O glorious day of eternity, on which night never throws its shadows, and whose perpetual light is the Sovereign Truth! O day of unending gladness, and of everlasting and unchanging security! How greatly I long for the dawning of this day, and the end of all worldly things. On the Saints this day already shines, resplendent with everlasting glory;

1. Isa. xxv, 8.   3. Heb. x, 32; xi, 34.   5. John xiv, 3.
2. Wisd. iii, 1; v, 16. 4. Rev. xiv, 13.   6. Rev. xxi, 2.

but to us who are pilgrims on earth[1] it appears but dim and
distant. The citizens of Heaven now taste the joys of this
day; but we, exiled children of Eve, mourn our bitterness
and weariness, for the days of this life are short and evil, full
of grief and pain.[2] Here man is defiled by many sins, ensnared by many passions, a prey to countless fears. Racked
by many cares, and distracted by many strange things, he is
entangled in many vanities. He is hedged in by many errors,
worn out by many labours, burdened by temptations,
enervated by pleasures, tormented by want.

Oh, when will all these evils come to an end? When shall
I be set free from the unhappy slavery of sin? When, O
Lord, shall my mind be fixed on You alone?[3] When shall
the fullness of your joys be mine? When shall I enjoy true
freedom, untrammelled and untroubled in mind or body?
When shall true peace be established – peace untroubled and
secure, peace both inward and outward, peace in every way
assured? Good Jesus, when shall I stand in Your presence?
When shall I see the glory of Your Kingdom? When will
You be All in all to me?[4] When shall I dwell with You in
Your Kingdom, which You have prepared from eternity
for those whom You love?[5]

I am left exiled and destitute in the land of my enemies,
where there are daily wars and awful calamities. Give me
comfort in my banishment, and ease my grief, for my whole
desire and longing is for You alone. Everything that this
world offers me as comfort is utterly distasteful; I long for
close communion with You, but cannot attain to it. I wish
to hold fast to heavenly things, but worldly affairs and
desires that I cannot master hold me down. I wish my mind
to rise freely above all these things, but my body holds me

1. Heb. xi, 13; I Cor. xiii, 12.   2. Job vii, 6.   3. Ps. lxxi, 16.
4. I Cor. xv, 28; Col. iii, 11.   5. Matt. xxv, 34.

its unwilling captive. Thus I struggle unhappily with myself: I am a burden to myself, for while my spirit longs to mount heavenwards, my body desires to remain below.

Oh, how deep is my pain! For whenever I try to contemplate heavenly things, a flood of worldly thoughts at once pours in upon me as I pray. My God, do not desert me! Do not abandon me in Your anger.[1] Strike with Your lightning, and scatter them: loose Your arrows[2] at the enemy, and utterly defeat all his wiles. Recall all my senses to Yourself, and cause me to forget all worldly things: help me to reject with scorn all the promptings of vice.

O Everlasting Truth, come to my aid, and let not vanity move me. Come, O delight of Heaven, and put to flight every impure thing! Grant me pardon, and in Your mercy deal kindly with me whenever I think of anything but Yourself at prayer; for I freely confess that I am usually beset by many distractions. Often, indeed, I do not really remain in my body at all, but am carried away by my thoughts. Where my thoughts come to rest, there am I, and my thoughts are most frequently with the things I love. For whatever is either delightful of itself, or has become pleasant through custom comes readily to the mind.

It is for this reason that You, who are the Truth, have plainly said, 'Where your treasure is, there will your heart be also.'[3] If I love Heaven, I think readily of heavenly things. If I love the world, I take pleasure in the delights of the world, and grieve in its troubles. If I love my body, my imagination dwells often on the things of the body. If I love the spirit, I love to think on the things of the spirit. For whatever things I love, it is of these that I am eager to speak and hear, and I have these interests always at heart.

Blessed is the man who for Your sake, Lord, bids farewell

1. Ps. xxv, 16; lxxi, 12.   2. Ps. cxliv, 6.   3. Matt. vi, 21.

to every creature, and, forcibly overcoming his natural inclinations, crucifies the desires of the flesh by the very fervour of his spirit,[1] in order that he may offer You pure prayer with a quiet conscience. Having excluded all worldly things from his heart and life, he will be worthy to take his place in the choir of Angels.

CHAPTER 49

On the Desire for Eternal Life, and the Wonder of God's Promises

CHRIST. My son, when you realize the heavenly origin of your desire for eternal blessedness, and long to escape from the prison of the body in order to be able to contemplate My unchanging glory,[2] then open your heart, and eagerly receive this holy inspiration. Offer fervent thanks for My divine generosity, that deals with you so kindly, visits you with mercy, inflames you to ardour, and powerfully supports you lest your own nature cause you to relapse into worldliness. It is not by any resolution or effort of your own that you receive this gift, but solely by the favour and grace of Heaven and God's regard. It is granted that you may grow in virtue and in deeper humility, and may prepare yourself for further conflicts, striving with whole-hearted devotion to hold fast to Me, and serve Me with sincere goodwill.

Son, there are many fires, but the flame never ascends unaccompanied by smoke. Similarly, the desires of some are afire for heavenly things, while they themselves are not yet free from the lusts of the flesh. Therefore they do not act solely for the glory of God when they make such earnest requests of Him. And your own desires, which you think so

1. Gal. v, 24.   2. John xvii, 24.

sincere, are often like this. For no desires are pure and perfect that are tainted by self-interest.

Do not ask for what is pleasant and profitable to yourself, but what is acceptable to Me and tends to My glory; for if you view things in their proper light, you will prefer and follow My direction rather than your own desires, whatever they may be. I know your desire, and have often heard your cry. You long for the glorious liberty of the sons of God,[1] while your eternal home and the joys of the heavenly country already draw your heart. But the time for this has not yet come; there remains warfare, work, and trial. You desire to be filled with the supreme Good, but you cannot attain this blessing now. I am that Good; wait for Me, says the Lord, until the coming of the Kingdom of God.

You must still be proved in this life, and many trials await you. Consolation will sometimes be granted you, but not in its fullness. So be strong and courageous,[2] both in doing and enduring what by nature is repugnant to you. It is necessary for you to become a new man,[3] and to be changed into another person.[4] It is often your duty to act against your own inclination, and to set aside your own wishes. The affairs of others may prosper, while your own wishes are frustrated. The words of others will be listened to, while yours will be disregarded. Others will ask and receive their request, while you ask and receive nothing. Others will be highly commended, while you remain unrecognized. Others will be entrusted with this or that office, while you are not considered suitable for anything. Your nature will cry out at this treatment, but it will be a great achievement if you remain silent, for in these and similar ways the faithful servant of our Lord is tested, that he may learn to deny and subdue himself in everything. There is

1. Rom. viii, 21.   3. Eph. iv, 24.
2. Joshua i, 7.   4. 1 Sam. x, 6.

hardly anything in which we have such need to die to self as in seeing and suffering things that are contrary to our wishes, especially when we are ordered to do what appears inconvenient and useless. And because, being under authority, you do not presume to resist the higher power, it seems a hardship to bow to the will of another, and to yield your own opinion.

Consider the results of your work, My son; its approaching end, and its boundless reward. Then it will not make you unhappy, but powerfully strengthen your resolution. In return for the surrender of your own will, you shall always have your will in Heaven. There you will find all that you wish, all that you can desire; there you will enjoy all good things without fear of loss. There your own will shall always be in accord with Mine, and you will desire no personal good, but Myself. None will oppose you there, none complain of you, obstruct or thwart you. Everything that you desire will be at hand, and will stimulate your love and fill it to overflowing. There you will receive glory in return for insults suffered here; a robe of honour[1] instead of grief, and in return for your humble place on earth a throne in My heavenly Kingdom. There will the fruit of your obedience appear, your acts of penance be turned to joy, and your former humble subjection be crowned with glory.

For the present, then, bear yourself humbly towards all men, and do not mind who it is that speaks or commands; but take care that whether it be your superior, your inferior or your equal who makes any request or suggestion, you take it all in good part, and sincerely try to fulfil their wish. Let men seek many different things, one making pleasure in this, another in that, and being highly commended for it. For your part, take pleasure in none of these things, but in the humble esteem of yourself and in My good pleasure and

1. Isa. lxi, 3.

honour alone. Let this be your constant desire – that, whether in life or death, God may at all times be glorified in you.[1]

CHAPTER 50

On Trust in God in all Trouble

THE DISCIPLE. O Lord God, heavenly Father, blessed be Your Name for ever. As You decree, so it is done, and whatever You do is always good. Let all my joy depend on You, not on myself or on any other thing, for I am Your servant. You alone are my true joy, Lord; my hope and my crown, my gladness and my honour. I, Your servant, possess nothing that is not Your gift, and have no merit of my own.[2] All things are Yours, both what You have given, and what You have created. I am poor and in trouble from my youth up,[3] and my soul is often distressed to the point of tears; sometimes, too, it is oppressed by the sufferings that beset me. I long for the joys of Your peace, and I pray most earnestly for the peace of Your children, who are refreshed in the light of Your comfort. Give me this peace, and fill my heart with holy joy; then will the soul of Your servant be full of song and entirely devoted to Your praise. But when You withdraw Yourself, as You often do, I cannot follow the way of Your commandments.[4] Instead, I fall on my knees and beat my breast, because things are not with me as they formerly were, when Your light shone upon my head,[5] and I was protected under the shadow of Your wings[6] from the temptations that assailed me.

O righteous Father, ever to be praised, now is the hour of Your servant's trial. Father, worthy of all love, it is right

1. Phil. i, 20.　　3. Ps. lxxxviii, 15.　　5. Job xxix, 3.
2. 1 Cor. iv, 7.　　4. Ps. cxix, 35.　　6. Ps. xvii, 8.

that I should now suffer something for Your sake. O Father, ever to be honoured, the hour has come[1] which has lain in Your foreknowledge from all eternity, when for a while Your servant will seem utterly defeated; yet let him inwardly feel Your presence. He will be maligned and humiliated, a failure in the eyes of men, broken by suffering and sickness, that with You he may rise again in the light of a new dawn, and receive glory in Heaven. This, most holy Father, is by Your appointment, and all is done as You have ordained.

To Your friends You grant this favour, that for love of You, they endure every trouble that You allow to come upon them, for nothing can happen in this world without Your foreknowledge and consent. Lord, it is good for me that You have humbled me, that I may learn Your justice,[2] and banish all conceit and presumption from my heart. It is good for me that I have suffered humiliation,[3] that I may seek comfort in Yourself rather than in men. Thus have I learned to stand in awe of Your unsearchable judgements, who correct both the just and the wicked with equity and justice.

I thank You that You have not spared my wrongdoing, but have punished me with bitter pain, inflicted sorrow on me, and sent me troubles of every kind. Nothing under heaven can comfort me but You alone, O Lord my God, for You are the heavenly Physician of souls, who both wound and heal, who cast down and raise up again.[4] Your discipline corrects me, and Your very scourge will heal me.[5]

Most loving Father, I place myself entirely in Your hands. I submit to Your correction; strike me, until my wayward stubbornness yields to Your will. Make me Your true and humble disciple, as You are wont to do, that I may serve

1. John xvi, 32.   3. Ps. lxix, 7.   5. Ps. xviii, 35.
2. Ps. cxix, 71.   4. 1 Sam. ii, 6.

Your good pleasure in all things. To Your correction, Lord, I deliver myself and all I am; for it is better to be punished in this life than the next. All things lie within Your knowledge, and nothing in the conscience of man is hid from Your eyes. You know all things before they come to pass, and need no man to inform You of the happenings of this earth. You know what is needful to my progress, and how well trouble serves to scour away the rust of my wickedness. Do with me according to Your good pleasure, and do not reject my sinful life, known to none more fully and clearly than Yourself.

Grant me, Lord, to know all that I should know, to love what I should love, to esteem what most pleases You, and to reject all that is evil in Your sight. Let me not judge superficially by what I see, nor be influenced by what I hear from ignorant men, but with true judgement to discern between things spiritual and material, and to seek Your will and good pleasure at all times and above all else.

The mind of man is often deceived in its judgement, and worldly men are deceived in their concern for material things alone. Is any man made the better for being highly honoured by his fellows? When one man flatters another, then one deceiver deceives another; the vain deceives the vain, the weak deceives the weak; and the higher the flattery, the deeper the shame it brings in its train. For, 'what every man is in Your sight, O Lord, that he is and nothing more', says the humble Saint Francis.[1]

1. S. Bonaventura, *Life of S. Francis*, Ch. vi.

CHAPTER 51

How when we Lack Strength for Higher Work
we should Undertake Humble Tasks

CHRIST. My Son, you cannot always burn with zeal for virtue, nor remain constantly in high contemplation; the weakness of sinful human nature will at times compel you to descend to lesser things, and bear with sorrow the burdens of this present life. So long as you wear this mortal body, you will be subject to weariness and sadness of heart. Therefore, in this life, you will often lament the burden of the body, which hinders your giving yourself wholly to the life of the spirit and to divine contemplation.

When this happens, you will be wise to resort to humble, exterior tasks, and to restore yourself by good works. Await My coming with unshakeable trust, and bear your exile and desolation of spirit with patience until I come again and set you free from all anxiety. Then you will forget all your former toil, and will enjoy inward peace. I will unfold before you the fair fields of the Scriptures, and you shall advance in the way of My commandments with heart at liberty.[1] Then you shall say, 'The sufferings of this present time are not worthy to be compared with the glory that shall be revealed in us.'[2]

CHAPTER 52

How no Man is Worthy of God's Comfort

THE DISCIPLE. Lord, I am not worthy of Your comfort, nor of any spiritual consolation. You deal justly with me when You leave me poor and desolate. Could I shed a sea of tears, I should still not deserve Your comfort. I merit nothing but

1. Ps. cxix, 32.   2. Rom. viii, 18.

scourging and punishment, for I have gravely and frequently offended You, and have done much evil. All things considered, therefore, I do not deserve the smallest consolation. Yet, most gracious and merciful God, You do not will that any of Your creatures should perish. Desiring to show Your generosity and goodness to those who receive Your mercy,[1] You reach down to comfort Your servant above his deserts, and in ways above man's knowledge; for Your consolation is not as the empty words of men.

What have I done, that You should grant me any comfort from heaven? I cannot recall any good that I have done, but have been ever prone to sin, and slow to amend. This is the truth, and I cannot deny it. If I pleaded otherwise, You would confront me, and none could defend me. What have I deserved for my sins, but hell and everlasting fire? I sincerely confess that I am fit only for scorn and contempt; I am unfit to be counted among Your faithful servants.

Although it pains me to repeat it, yet for truth's sake I will accuse myself, that I may better deserve Your mercy. Guilty and confused, what shall I say? I can but say, 'I have sinned, O Lord,[2] I have sinned; be merciful and forgive. Spare me awhile, that I may show my sorrow, before I go down into the darkness and shadow of death.'[3] Why do You demand of a guilty and wretched sinner that he repent and humble himself for his offences? It is because in true penitence and humbleness of heart is born the hope of pardon; the troubled conscience is reconciled; lost grace restored; man is spared the anger of God;[4] while God and the penitent soul greet each other in a holy embrace.[5] Humble sorrow for sin is an acceptable sacrifice to You, Lord, and is more fragrant in Your sight than clouds of incense. This is the precious ointment which You once allowed to be poured on Your

1. Rom. ix, 23.   3. Job x, 21.   5. Rom. xvi, 16.
2. Ps. li, 3.   4. Matt. iii, 7.

sacred feet;[1] for You have never despised a contrite and humble heart.[2] Here at Your feet is the place of refuge from the hatred of the Enemy; here is the place of amendment and cleansing from every stain of sin.

CHAPTER 53

How God's Grace is not Granted to the Worldly-Minded

CHRIST. My son, My grace is precious, and may not be mingled with worldly concerns and pleasures. Therefore, if you wish to receive it, you must remove every obstacle to grace. Seek out a place apart, and love the solitary life. Do not engage in conversation with men, but instead pour forth devout prayer to God, that you may preserve a humble mind and a clean conscience. Count the whole world as nothing, and place attendance on God before all outward things. For you cannot attend on Me, and at the same time take pleasure in worldly things. Remain detached from acquaintances and friends and independent of this world's consolations. It is for this reason that the blessed Apostle Peter begs all the faithful in Christ to keep themselves as strangers and pilgrims in this world.[3]

With what confidence will a man meet death, to whom no worldly affection clings! But a weak soul cannot bear to be thus detached from all things, nor can a worldly-minded man understand the freedom of the spiritual man.[4] Nevertheless, when a man sincerely desires to be spiritual, he must renounce all, both friend and stranger, and must beware of none more than himself. If you can win complete mastery over self, you will easily master all else. To triumph over self is the perfect victory. For whoever so controls himself

1. Luke vii, 46. 3. I Pet. ii, 11.
2. Ps. li, 17. 4. I Cor. ii, 14.

that his passions are subject to his reason, and his reason wholly subject to Me, is master both of himself and of the world.

If you aspire to reach this height of perfection, you must make a brave beginning. Lay the axe to the roots,[1] to cut out and destroy all inordinate and secret love of self, and of any personal and material advantage. From this vice of inordinate self-love spring nearly all those other failings that have to be completely overcome. But as soon as this evil is mastered and subdued, great peace and lasting tranquillity will follow. But few endeavour to die completely to self, and to rise wholly above it; consequently, they remain absorbed in themselves, and quite unable to rise in spirit above self. He who desires to walk with Me in true freedom must mortify all irregular and undisciplined desires, and have no selfish longing for any creature.

CHAPTER 54
On the Contrary Workings of Nature and Grace

CHRIST. My son, carefully observe the impulses of nature and grace, for these are opposed one to another, and work in so subtle a manner that even a spiritual, holy and enlightened man can hardly distinguish them. All men do in fact desire what is good, and in what they say and do pretend to some kind of goodness, so that many are deceived by their appearance of virtue.

Nature is crafty, and seduces many, snaring and deceiving them, and always works for her own ends. But Grace moves in simplicity, avoiding every appearance of evil. She makes no attempt to deceive, and does all things purely for love of God, in whom she rests as her final goal.

1. Matt. iii, 10; Luke iii, 9.

Nature is unwilling to be mortified, checked or over-come, obedient or willingly subject. Grace mortifies herself, resists sensuality, submits to control, seeks to be overcome. She does not aim at enjoying her own liberty, but loves to be under discipline; and does not wish to lord it over any-one. Rather does she desire to live, abide and exist always under God's rule, and for His sake she is ever ready to submit it to all men.[1]

Nature works for her own interest, and estimates what profit she may derive from others. Grace does not consider what may be useful or convenient to herself, but only what may be to the good of many.[2] Nature is eager to receive honour and reward: Grace faithfully ascribes all honour and glory to God.[3] Nature fears shame and con-tempt: Grace is glad to suffer reproach for the Name of Jesus.[4] Nature loves ease and rest for the body; Grace cannot be idle, but welcomes work cheerfully.

Nature loves to enjoy rare and beautiful things, and hates the cheap and clumsy. Grace takes pleasure in simple and humble things, neither despising the rough, nor refusing to wear the old and ragged. Nature pays regard to temporal affairs, takes pleasure in this world's wealth, grieves at any loss, and is angered by a slighting remark. But Grace pays attention to things eternal, and is not attached to the temporal. The loss of goods fails to move her, or hard words to anger her, for she lays up her treasure and joy in Heaven where none of it can be lost.[5]

Nature is greedy, and grasps more readily than she gives, loving to retain things for her personal use. But Grace is kind and generous, shuns private interest, is contented with little, and esteems it more blest to give than to receive.[6] Nature inclines a man towards creatures – to the body, to

1. 1 Pet. ii, 13.   3. Ps. xxix, 2; xcvi, 7.   5. Matt. vi, 20.
2. 1 Cor. x, 33.   4. Acts v, 41.   6. Acts xx, 35.

vanities, to restlessness. But Grace draws a man towards God and virtue. Renouncing creatures, she flees the world, loathes the lusts of the flesh, limits her wanderings, and shuns public appearances. Nature is eager to enjoy any outward comfort that will gratify the senses. Grace seeks comfort in God alone, and delights in the Sovereign Good above all visible things.

Nature does everything for her own gain and interest; she does nothing without fee, hoping either to obtain some equal or greater return for her services, or else praise and favour. But Grace seeks no worldly return, and asks for no reward, but God alone. She desires no more of the necessaries of life than will serve her to obtain the things of eternity.

Nature takes pleasure in a host of friends and relations; she boasts of noble rank and high birth; makes herself agreeable to the powerful, flatters the rich, and acclaims those who are like herself. But Grace loves even her enemies,[1] takes no pride in the number of her friends, and thinks little of high birth unless it be allied to the greater virtue. She favours the poor rather than the rich, and has more in common with the honourable than with the powerful. She takes pleasure in an honest man, not in a deceiver; she constantly encourages good men to labour earnestly for the better gifts,[2] and by means of these virtues to become like the Son of God.

Nature is quick to complain of want and hardship; but Grace bears poverty with courage. Nature, struggling and striving on her own behalf, turns everything to her own interest: but Grace refers all things to God, from whom they come. She attributes no good to herself; she is not arrogant and presumptuous. She does not argue and exalt her own opinions before others, but submits all her powers

1. Matt. v, 44; Luke vi, 27.   2. I. Cor. xii, 31.

of mind and perception to the eternal wisdom and judgement of God. Nature is curious to know secrets and to hear news; she loves to be seen in public, and to enjoy sensations. She desires recognition, and to do such things as win praise and admiration. But Grace does not care for news or novelties, because all these things spring from the age-old corruption of man, for there is nothing new or lasting in this world.

Grace therefore teaches us how the senses are to be disciplined and vain complacency avoided; how anything likely to excite praise and admiration should be humbly concealed; and how in all things and in all knowledge some useful fruit should be sought, together with the praise and honour of God. She wants no praise for herself or her doings, but desires that God may be blessed in His gifts, who out of pure love bestows all things.

Grace is a supernatural light, and the especial gift of God,[1] the seal of His chosen and the pledge of salvation,[2] which raises man from earthly things to love the heavenly, and from worldly makes him spiritual. The more, therefore, that Nature is controlled and overcome, the richer is the grace bestowed, while man is daily renewed by fresh visitations after the likeness of God.[3]

CHAPTER 55
On the Corruption of Nature, and the Power of Grace

THE DISCIPLE. O Lord my God, You have created me in Your own image and likeness. Grant me this great grace, so necessary to my salvation, that I may conquer the base elements of my nature,[4] that drag me down into sin and

1. Eph. ii, 8.　　3. Col. iii, 10.
2. Eph. i, 14.　　4. Rom. vii, 23.

perdition. Within my being I can feel the power of sin contending against the rule of my mind, leading me away an obedient slave to all kinds of sensuality. I cannot resist its onslaughts, unless Your most holy grace is poured glowing into my heart to help me.

I need Your grace in fullest measure, to subdue that nature which always inclines to evil from my youth up.[1] For it fell through Adam the first of men, and was tainted by sin, the penalty of that fault descending upon all mankind. Thus the nature which You created good and upright has now become the very symbol of corruption and weakness, for when left to itself, it leans always towards evil and base things. The little strength that remains is only like a small spark, buried beneath ashes. Yet this same natural reason, though hidden in profound darkness, still retains the power to know good and evil, and to discern truth and falsehood. But it is powerless to do what it knows to be good, neither does it enjoy the full light of truth, nor its former healthy affections.

Thus, O Lord my God, it comes about that, while I inwardly delight in Your law,[2] and know Your commands to be good, just, and holy,[3] both for the condemnation of all evil and the avoiding of sin, yet in my body I serve the law of sin,[4] and obey my senses before my reason. Hence, while I indeed possess the will to good, I find myself powerless to follow it.[5] In this way, I make many good resolutions, but, through lack of grace to support my weakness, any small obstacle causes discouragement and failure. Thus, too, I know the way of perfection, and see clearly enough what I ought to do; but I am borne down by the burden of my own corruption, and advance no nearer to perfection.

Lord, how urgently I need Your grace if I am to under-

1. Gen. viii, 21. 3. Rom. vii, 12. 5. Rom. vii, 18.
2. Rom. vii, 22. 4. Rom. vii, 25.

take, carry out and perfect any good work! Without it, I can achieve nothing; but in You and by the power of Your grace, all things are possible.[1] O true and heavenly grace, without which our own merits are nothing, and our natural gifts of no account! Neither arts nor riches, beauty nor strength, genius nor eloquence have any value in Your eyes, Lord, unless allied to grace. For the gifts of nature are common to good men and bad alike, but grace or love are Your especial gift to those whom You choose, and those who are sealed with this are counted worthy of life everlasting. So excellent is this grace that neither the gift of prophecy, nor the working of miracles, nor any speculation, however sublime, is of any value without it. Indeed, not even faith, or hope, or any other virtue is acceptable to You without love and grace.

O most blessed grace, that makes the poor in spirit rich in virtues, and the richly blessed humble in heart! Come, descend on me! Fill me with your comfort,[2] lest my soul faint from weariness and dryness of mind. I pray, Lord, that I may find favour in Your sight, for Your grace is sufficient for me,[3] even if I obtain none of those things that nature desires. However often I am tempted and troubled, I will fear no evil[4] so long as Your grace remains with me.

Your grace is my strength, my counsel, and my help. It is more powerful than all my enemies, and wiser than all the wise. It is the teacher of truth, the instructor of doctrine, the light of the heart, the consoler of affliction. It banishes sorrow, drives away fear, fosters devotion, and moves to contrition. Without grace, I am nothing but a dry tree, a barren stock[5] fit only for destruction. Therefore, O Lord, let Your grace always lead and follow me,[6] and keep me ever intent on good works, through Your Son Jesus Christ. Amen.

1. Phil. iv, 13.   3. 2 Cor. xii, 9.   5. Ecclus. vi, 3.
2. Ps. xc, 14.   4. Ps. xxiii, 4.   6. Collect, Trinity xvii.

CHAPTER 56

How we must Follow Christ's Way of the Cross in Self-Denial

CHRIST. My son, you will be able to enter into Me in so far as you are prepared to forsake yourself. And as the absence of craving for material things makes for inner peace, so does the forsaking of self unite man's heart to God. I wish you to learn perfect self-surrender, and to accept My will without argument or complaint. Follow me,[1] who am the Way, the Truth and the Life.[2] Without the Way, there is no progress; without the Truth, there is no knowledge; without the Life, there is no living. I am the Way you must follow; the Truth you must believe; the Life for which you must hope. I am the imperishable Way, the infallible Truth, the eternal Life. I am the most noble Way, the ultimate Truth, the true Life, blessed and uncreated. If you remain in My Way, you shall know the Truth, and the Truth shall set you free,[3] and you shall lay hold on eternal Life.[4]

If you wish to enter into Life, keep My Commandments.[5] If you wish to know the Truth, believe Me. If you wish to be perfect, sell everything.[6] If you wish to be My disciple, deny yourself.[7] If you wish to possess the blessed Life, despise this present life. If you wish to be exalted in Heaven, be humble in this world. If you wish to reign with Me, bear the cross with Me; for none but the servants of the Cross discover the Way of blessedness and true light.

THE DISCIPLE. Lord Jesus, just as Your brief life was despised by the world, grant that I may follow You in bearing the world's contempt. For the servant is not greater than his master, nor is the pupil superior to his teacher.[8] Let Your servant be instructed in Your life, for it is the source of

1. Matt. ix, 9.
2. John xiv, 6.
3. John viii, 32.
4. John viii, 12; 1 Tim. vi, 12.
5. Matt. xix, 17.
6. Matt. xix, 21.
7. Matt. xvi, 24.
8. Matt. x, 24.

salvation and true holiness. Whatever I study or hear beside this affords me neither new strength nor fullest joy.

CHRIST. My son, since you know and have studied these things, blessed are you if you do them.[1] Whoever truly loves Me knows and obeys My commands. I will love him, and will reveal Myself to him,[2] and he shall reign with Me in the Kingdom of My Father.[3]

THE DISCIPLE. Lord Jesus, let it be as You have said; and may I merit the fulfilment of Your promise. I have accepted the Cross from Your own hands: as You have laid it upon me, I have accepted it, and will bear it until death. The life of a good Religious is truly a cross, but it is also our guide to Paradise. We have begun; we may not turn back, nor can we abandon it. Up, then, my brothers! Let us go forward together! Jesus will be with us. For Jesus' sake, we have taken up the cross; for Jesus' sake, let us persevere in it. He will be our helper, who is also our leader; He has gone before us. See, our King advances in the vanguard, and will fight for us! Let us follow like men; no terrors shall daunt us. We must be ready to die bravely in battle,[4] and never tarnish our glory[5] by deserting the Cross.

CHAPTER 57
That we should never Despair

CHRIST. My son, patience and humility in adversity are more pleasing to Me than great devotion and comfort in times of ease. Why are you so distressed when you are criticized in some small matter? Had it been a far more serious matter, that is no reason for your being disturbed. Let it pass. It is not your first mistake, or anything new; nor, if you live

1. John xiii, 17.   3. Rev. iii, 21.   5. 1 Macc. ix, 10.
2. John xiv, 21.   4. 1 Macc. iii, 59.

long, will it be your last. You are brave enough when you meet no opposition. You can give good advice and encouragement to others, but when trouble knocks unexpectedly at your own door, your strength and judgement fail you. Remember the great weakness you often experience in small troubles; yet these things happen for your own good.

Banish discouragement from your heart as best you can, and if trouble comes, never let it depress or hinder you for long. At the least, bear it bravely if you cannot bear it cheerfully. Even if you are reluctant to bear it, and feel indignant, yet control yourself, and let no rash words escape you that may harm Christ's little ones. The violence of your feelings will soon subside, and grace return to heal your inner pain. 'I live,'[1] says the Lord, 'ready to help and comfort you more than ever, if you will trust Me and call on Me with devotion.'

Be of good heart,[2] and steel yourself to endure greater trials. All is not lost, however often you feel tempted or sorely troubled. You are a man, not God; you are human, not an angel. How can you expect to remain always in a constant state of virtue, when this was not possible even for an angel of Heaven, nor for the first man in the Garden? I am He who grants healing and comfort to those in distress,[3] and I raise up to My Divinity those who acknowledge their weakness.

THE DISCIPLE. Lord, blessed are Your words! They are sweeter to my mouth than honey and the honeycomb.[4] What would I do in such trials and troubles as mine, if You did not uphold me with Your holy words? So long as I come at last to the haven of salvation, what matters the kind or magnitude of my sufferings? Grant me a holy

1. Isa. xlix, 18.   3. Job v, 11.
2. Baruch iv, 30.   4. Ps. xix, 10; cxix, 103.

end, and a joyful passing out of this world. Remember me, O my God, and lead me in the right way to Your Kingdom.

CHAPTER 58

How we may not Inquire into the Unsearchable
Judgements of God

CHRIST. My son, avoid controversy over high things and the judgements of God. Do not argue why this person is so forsaken while another is endowed with great graces; or why one person is so grievously afflicted, while another is so richly rewarded. These things are above human understanding, and neither reasoning nor argument is competent to explain the judgements of God. Therefore, when the enemy suggests these things to your mind, or when inquisitive people ask about them, answer with the prophet, 'You are just, O Lord, and Your judgements are right.'[1] My judgements are to be respected, not discussed, for they are beyond the comprehension of the human mind.[2]

Do not dispute over the merits of the Saints, which is the holier, or which the greater in the Kingdom of Heaven. This often breeds strife and unprofitable arguments,[3] feeding pride and empty boasting, from which in turn spring envy and dissension, while one proudly seeks to praise this Saint, and another that. Now, this desire to know and explore such matters is unprofitable, and is displeasing to the Saints themselves. 'I am not the God of dissension, but of peace',[4] and My peace is founded on humility, not on self-exaltation.

Some, in their ardent enthusiasm, profess a greater devotion to one Saint than to another; but this devotion is

1. Ps. cxix, 137.   3. 2 Tim. ii, 23.
2. Rom. xi, 33.   4. 1 Cor. xiv, 33.

of human origin, not divine. I am He who made all the Saints; I gave them grace; I endowed them with glory. I know the merits of each; I went before them with My blessings.[1] I foreknew my loved ones before time began.[2] I chose them out of the world;[3] they did not first choose Me. I called them by grace;[4] I drew them by mercy. I was their guide in many a temptation; I poured forth on them wonderful consolations. I gave them perseverance, and I crowned their patience.

I know them, the first and the last, and enfold them all in My boundless love. I am to be praised in all My Saints. I am to be blessed above all things, and to be honoured in each of these, whom I have predestinated and raised to such glory with no previous merits of their own. Anyone, therefore, who disparages one of the least[5] of My Saints, in no way adds to the glory of a greater by so doing, for small and great alike are My creation.[6] And any who speaks lightly of any of the Saints, speaks lightly both of Myself and of all the company of Heaven. All are one in the bond of charity; their thoughts and aspirations are one, and all love each other as one.[7]

But this is higher still, that they love Me more than themselves and their own merits. Caught up out of themselves, and carried beyond love of self, they are wholly engaged in loving me, in whom they rest in peace and joy. Nothing can distract or dismay them, for they are full of the eternal Truth, and burn with the fire of unquenchable charity. Let base and worldly men therefore refrain from dispute about the state of the Saints, for such men care for nothing but their own gratification. In their own interest, they exaggerate or belittle facts, and pay no regard to the

1. Ps. xxi, 3.   4. Gal. i, 15.   6. Wisd. vi, 7.
2. Rom. viii, 29.   5. Matt. xviii, 10.   7. John xvii, 21.
3. John xv, 19.

178

eternal Truth. In the case of many, it is through ignorance, especially in those who are but little enlightened, and are seldom capable of loving anyone with a perfect and spiritual love. Such people are still strongly attracted to one person or another by natural affection and human friendship; and as they behave towards men on earth, so do they imagine that they can regard the Saints in Heaven. But the thoughts of imperfect men are immeasurably below those implanted in the enlightened by the revelations of God.

Beware, therefore, My son, of being over curious about matters beyond your knowledge; let your aim and object rather be to be counted even among the least in the Kingdom of God. Even if a man could know who is the holiest and greatest in the Kingdom of Heaven, of what use could this knowledge be, unless it led him to humble himself before Me, and rise up to praise My Name with increased devotion? It is far more acceptable to God that a man consider the enormity of his own sins, the smallness of his virtue, and how far he is from the perfection of the Saints, than that he should dispute who is the greater or lesser among them. It is better to supplicate the Saints with devout prayer and sorrow, and to implore their glorious prayers, than to search into their secrets with vain curiosity.

The Saints enjoy a good and perfect contentment; ah, if only men could be content, and control their empty talk! The Saints do not boast of their own merits; they ascribe no goodness to themselves, but all to Me, for I gave them everything out of My boundless love. They are filled by so deep a love for God, and with so overflowing a joy, that nothing is wanting to their glory, nor can anything be lacking in their happiness. The higher they stand in glory, the more humble are the Saints in themselves, and the closer they are to Me, and better loved. Thus you have the scripture, 'They cast down their crowns before God, and fell on their faces before the Lamb; and they adored Him who lives for ever and ever.'[1]

Many ask, 'Who is the greatest in the Kingdom of Heaven?'[2] not knowing whether they themselves will ever be counted even the least in it. It is a great thing to be even the least in Heaven, where all are great, for all shall be called the children of God,[3] and shall truly be so. The least shall be valued as a thousand, the sinner, though he be an hundred years old, shall perish.[4] When the disciples inquired who should be the greater in the Kingdom of Heaven, they received this reply: 'Unless you be converted, and become as little children, you shall not enter the Kingdom of Heaven. Therefore, whosoever shall humble himself as this little child shall be the greater in the Kingdom of Heaven.'[5]

Woe to those who are too proud readily to humble themselves like little children, for the humble gates of Heaven will not open to admit them. Woe also to the rich, who enjoy their pleasures in this life;[6] for while the poor enter into the Kingdom of God, they shall stand weeping outside. Be glad, you humble! Leap for joy, O poor! The Kingdom of God is yours if you will but live in the Truth.[7]

CHAPTER 59
That we should Hope and Trust in God Alone

THE DISCIPLE. Lord, in what can I trust in this life? And what is my greatest comfort on earth? Is it not Yourself, O Lord my God, whose mercy is limitless? Have I ever prospered without You? And did I ever suffer ill when You were at hand? I would rather be poor for Your sake than rich

1. Rev. iv, 10. 4. Isa. lx, 22; lxv, 20. 6. Luke vi, 24.
2. Matt. xviii, 1. 5. Matt. xviii, 3. 7. 2 John 4.
3. Matt. v, 9.

without You. I would choose to be a wanderer on the face of the earth with You, rather than to possess heaven without You. For where You are, there is Heaven; and where You are not, there is death and Hell. You are my sole desire; for You I sigh, pray, and cry. I cannot put all my trust in any mortal man to afford me help sufficient for my needs, but in You alone, O my God. You are my hope,[1] my trust, and my strength, most faithful in all things.

Men seek their own interest,[2] but You, Lord, seek only my salvation and welfare, and turn all things to my good.[3] Even when You expose me to various temptations and hardships, You order these entirely for my own good, for it is Your way to test Your chosen servants by many trials. During trials of this kind my love and praise is Your due no less than when You fill my soul with heavenly comfort.

It is in You, then, O Lord God, that I place my whole hope and trust. On You I lay all my trouble and distress; for wherever I look elsewhere, I find all things weak and unstable. The number of my friends will be unavailing; powerful allies will be unable to help; wise counsellors will not be able to give me a helpful answer, nor learned books give comfort; no precious substance can ransom me, nor can any secret and pleasant place afford refuge, unless You Yourself stand at my side to help me, to strengthen, cheer, instruct, and protect me.

Unless You abide with me, all things that seem to bring peace and happiness are as nothing, for they cannot bestow true happiness. You alone are the End of all good things, the fullness of life, the depth of wisdom; and the greatest comfort of Your servants is to trust in You above all else. My God, Father of mercies, I look to You, I trust in You.[4] Bless and hallow my soul with Your heavenly blessing, that it

1. Ps. xci, 2. 3. Rom. viii, 28.
2. Phil. ii, 21. 4. Ps. cxxiii, 1; cxli, 8.

may become Your holy dwelling and the seat of Your eternal glory. Let nothing remain in this temple of Your glory to offend the sight of Your divine majesty. Of Your great goodness and abundant mercy look on me and hear this prayer of Your humble servant, an exile from home in the land of the shadow of death.[1] Guard and preserve the soul of Your servant amid the many perils of this corruptible life. Let Your grace go with me, and guide me in the way of peace to my native land of perpetual light.

1. Ps. xxiii, 4; Isa. ix, 2.

BOOK FOUR

ON THE BLESSED SACRAMENT

The Voice of Christ

'COME TO ME, ALL WHO LABOUR AND ARE HEAVY LADEN, AND I WILL REFRESH YOU,' says the Lord.[1]

'THE BREAD THAT I WILL GIVE IS MY FLESH, FOR THE LIFE OF THE WORLD.'[2]

'TAKE AND EAT; THIS IS MY BODY WHICH SHALL BE OFFERED FOR YOU; DO THIS IN COMMEMORATION OF ME.'[3]

'WHOSOEVER EATS MY FLESH AND DRINKS MY BLOOD, DWELLS IN ME, AND I IN HIM.'[4] 'THESE THINGS THAT I HAVE TOLD YOU ARE SPIRIT AND LIFE.'[5]

CHAPTER I
On the Deep Reverence with which Christ should be Received

THE DISCIPLE. O Christ, Eternal Truth, these are Your own words, although not spoken all at one time or in one place. And since they are Your words, and are true, I must accept them with gratitude and trust. They are Your words, and You have spoken them; they are also mine, since You have given them to me for my salvation. Gladly do I receive them from Your lips, that they may be the more deeply

---

1. Matt. xi, 28.   3. Luke xxii, 19;   4. John vi, 56.
2. John vi, 51.   1 Cor. xi, 24.   5. John vi, 63.

imprinted in my heart. Your words, so tender, so full of sweetness and love, give me courage; but my own sins appal me, and a stricken conscience restrains me from receiving so high a Sacrament.

You command me to approach You in faith if I wish to have part in You, and to receive the food of immortality if I desire life and glory. 'Come to Me,' You say, 'all who labour and are heavy laden, and I will refresh you.' O Lord my God! How sweet and loving in the ears of a sinner are these words, with which You invite the poor and needy to the Communion of Your most holy Body! But who am I, O Lord, that I should presume to approach You? The very Heaven of Heavens cannot contain You;[1] and yet You say, 'Come you all to Me.'

What is the meaning of this kindly invitation? Unaware of any good in me on which I may presume, how shall I dare to come? How shall I invite You into my house, who have so often done evil in Your sight? The Angels and Archangels do You reverence; Saints and holy men stand in awe of You; yet You say, 'Come you all to Me'! Unless You Yourself had said it, who would believe it true? And who would dare approach, unless it were Your command?

Noah, a good man,[2] is said to have worked a hundred years to build the ark, so that he and a few others might be saved.[3] How, then, can I in one short hour prepare myself to receive with reverence the Creator of the world? Moses, Your great servant and especial friend, constructed an Ark of imperishable wood,[4] and covered it with purest gold, in order to house the Tablets of the Law: and how shall I, a corruptible creature, dare so lightly to receive You, the Maker of the Law and Giver of life? Solomon, wisest of

1. 1 Kings viii, 27.   3. 1 Pet. iii, 20.
2. Gen. vi, 9.   4. Exod. xxv, 10.

Israel's kings,[1] spent seven years in building a splendid Temple in praise of Your name. For eight days he kept the Feast of its Dedication, and offered a thousand peace-offerings. To the sound of trumpets, he solemnly and joyfully bore the Ark of the Covenant to its appointed resting-place. How, then, shall I, unworthiest and poorest of men, welcome You into my house,[2] when I can hardly spend half an hour devoutly? If only I could spend even half an hour as I ought!

O my God, how earnestly did all these strive to please You! And how little, alas, can I do! How short is the time that I employ in preparing myself for Communion! Seldom am I entirely recollected, and very seldom free from all distraction. Yet in Your saving presence, O God, no unbecoming thought should enter my mind, for it is not an Angel, but the Lord of Angels who comes to be my guest.

How great a difference there is between the Ark of the Covenant and its relics, and Your most holy Body with its ineffable powers: between those sacrifices of the old Law which foreshadowed the Sacrifice to come, and the true Victim of Your Body, which fulfils all the ancient rites!

Alas, why does not my heart burn within me at Your adorable presence? Why do I not prepare myself to receive Holy Communion, when the Patriarchs and Prophets of old, Kings and Princes with all their people, showed so great a devotion in Your holy worship?

The holy King David danced before the Ark with all his might,[3] recalling Your blessings to his fathers; he wrote psalms, and taught his people to sing with joy; inspired by the grace of the Holy Spirit, he often sang and played on the harp; he taught the people of Israel to praise God with the

1. 1 Kings v, 7.   3. 2 Sam. vi, 14.
2. Luke vii, 6.

whole heart, and to bless Him every day. If all these per-
formed such acts of praise and devotion before the Ark of
the Covenant, how much greater devotion and reverence
should I and all Christian people have in the presence of this
Sacrament, and in receiving the most adorable Body of
Christ?

Many make pilgrimages to various places to visit the relics
of the Saints, wondering at the story of their lives and the
splendour of their shrines; they view and venerate their
bones, covered with silks and gold. But here on the Altar
are You Yourself, my God, the Holy of Holies, Creator of
men and Lord of Angels! When visiting such places, men
are often moved by curiosity and the urge for sight-seeing,
and one seldom hears that any amendment of life results,
especially as their conversation is trivial and lacks true
contrition. But here, in the Sacrament of the Altar, You are
wholly present, my God, the Man Christ Jesus; here we
freely partake the fruit of eternal salvation, as often as we
receive You worthily and devoutly. No levity, curiosity, or
sentimentality must draw us, but firm faith, devout hope,
and sincere love.

O God, invisible Creator of the world, how wonderful
are Your dealings with us! How sweetly and graciously
You welcome Your chosen, to whom You give Yourself in
this Sacrament! It passes all understanding; it kindles the
love and draws the hearts of the faithful to Yourself. For
Your faithful ones, who strive to amend their whole lives,
receive in this most exalted Sacrament the grace of devotion
and the love of virtue.

O wonderful and hidden grace of this Sacrament, known
so well to Christ's faithful, but hidden from unbelievers and
servants of sin! In this Sacrament, spiritual grace is con-
veyed, lost virtue restored to the soul, and its sin-ravaged
beauty renewed. Such is the grace of this Sacrament, that

from the fullness of devotion You afford greater powers not only to the mind, but to the frail body.

We cannot but regret and deplore our own carelessness and tepidity, which hinders us from receiving Christ with greater love, for in Him rests all our merit and hope of salvation. He is our Sanctification[1] and Redemption: He is the comfort of pilgrims, and the everlasting joy of the Saints. How sad it is that so many have small regard for this saving Mystery, which is the delight of Heaven and preservative of the whole world. Alas, man is so blind, and his heart so hard, that he does not appreciate more fully this wonderful gift, and, from frequent use of it, grows even less reverent towards it!

If this most holy Sacrament were celebrated in one place only, and were offered by one priest only in the whole world, men would rush to this place and to the priest of God, to be present at the divine mysteries. But there are now many priests, and in many places Christ is offered, that the grace and love of God may be better known to men, the more widely Holy Communion is diffused through the world. O good Jesus, eternal Shepherd, we thank You that You deign to refresh us poor exiles with Your precious Body and Blood, and invite us to receive these Mysteries, saying, 'Come to Me, all who labour and are heavy laden, and I will refresh you.'

CHAPTER 2
On the Great Goodness and Love of God in this Sacrament

THE DISCIPLE. Trusting wholly in Your goodness and great mercy, Lord, I come sick to my Saviour, hungry and thirsty to the Fount of Life,[2] needy to the King of Heaven, a creature to its Creator, desolate to my loving Comforter.

1. 1 Cor. i, 30.   2. Ps. xxxvi, 9.

Yet whence is this favour, that You should come to me?[1] What am I, that You should give me Your very Self? How dare a sinner appear before You? And how is it that You deign to visit a sinner? You know Your servant, and see that he possesses no good in himself that could merit this blessing. Thus do I confess my worthlessness; I acknowledge Your goodness, I praise Your kindness, and I offer my gratitude for Your boundless love.[2] You do this of Your own will; not on account of my merits, but solely that Your goodness may be more evident to me, Your love more richly imparted to me, and that You may more perfectly commend humility to me. Therefore, since it is Your pleasure and You have thus commanded it, Your will is my delight; may no wickedness in me obstruct it.

O most kind and loving Jesus, what profound reverence, gratitude and eternal praise are Your due when we receive Your sacred Body; for none on earth can rightly extol Its majesty. What shall be my thoughts as I approach my Lord in Communion? I cannot pay Him the honour that is His due, and yet I desire to receive Him with devotion. What better or more salutary desire can I have than to humble myself completely before You, and to praise Your infinite goodness to me? Therefore, O my God, I offer You my praise, and will glorify You for ever, while in the depths of my insignificance I despise and abase myself in Your presence.

Lord, You are the Holy of Holies: I am the worst of sinners. Yet, O Lord, You stoop to me, who am not worthy even to raise my eyes towards You. Lord, You come to me, and desire to be with me; You invite me to Your Table; You wish to feed me with the Heavenly Food, the Bread of Angels. This Food is none other than Yourself, The Living Bread, who came down from Heaven to give life to the world.[3]

1. Luke i, 43.　　　2. Eph. ii, 4.　　　3. Ps. lxxviii, 25.

See, from whom this love proceeds! See the Source whence this high glory shines! How deep a gratitude, how high a praise are Your due for all these blessings! How greatly to our profit and salvation was Your counsel when You instituted this Sacrament! How sweet and delightful the Feast in which You give Yourself to be our food! How wonderful are Your ways, O Lord; how mighty Your power, how infallible Your truth! You spoke the word, and all things were made;[1] You commanded, and it was done.

It is indeed wonderful to consider, worthy of faith, and transcending the mind of man, how You, my Lord and God, true God and true man, are wholly present under the simple forms of bread and wine, and are eaten without being consumed by whoso receives You. O Lord of all things, who stand in need of none, and who yet are pleased to dwell[2] in us by means of this Sacrament; keep my heart and body spotless, that with a glad and pure conscience I may be enabled to celebrate Your holy Mysteries, and receive to my eternal salvation those things that You have hallowed and ordained to Your own especial honour and for Your perpetual memorial.

Be glad, my soul, and thank God for the noblest of all His gifts, for this unique comfort bestowed on you in this vale of tears. For as often as you consider this Mystery, and receive the Body of Christ, you set forward the work of your redemption, and become a sharer in all the merits of Christ. Therefore, continually dispose yourself to the renewal of your mind, and ponder deeply the great mystery of salvation. Whenever you celebrate or hear Mass, it should be as great, as fresh and as joyful to you as if on this very day Christ had come down for the first time into the womb of the Virgin, and was made man; or, hanging on the Cross, suffered and died for man's salvation.

1. Ps. cxlviii, 5.   2. 2 Macc. xiv, 35.

CHAPTER 3

On the Value of Frequent Communion

THE DISCIPLE. Lord, I come to You to receive the benefit of Your gift, and to enjoy the Feast that You have graciously prepared for the poor. In You I find all that I can or should desire; You are my Saviour and my Redeemer, my hopes and my strength, my honour and my glory. Therefore, Lord Jesus, gladden the soul of Your servant today, for to You I raise my soul.[1] I desire to receive You with reverence and devotion: I long to invite You into my house, that, like Zaccheus, I may win Your blessing and be numbered among Your chosen.[2] My soul longs to receive Your Body; my heart yearns to be united to You.

Give me Yourself, and it is enough; nothing but You can satisfy me. Without You I cannot exist; without Your visits I cannot live. Therefore I must often approach You, and receive You as the medicine of salvation, lest if I be deprived of this heavenly food, I faint by the way. For, O most merciful Jesus, it was Yourself who, when You had been preaching to the people and healing their many diseases, said, 'I will not send them away to their homes hungry, lest they faint on the way.'[3] Deal in like manner with me now, since You remain in this Sacrament for the comfort of the faithful. You are the sweet refreshment of the soul, and whoever receives You worthily will be a partaker and heir of eternal glory. It is essential to me, who am so prone to frequent falls, and who so quickly grow lukewarm and careless, that I renew, cleanse, and enkindle myself by frequent prayer and confession, and by the holy reception of Your Body; if I neglect these for long, I may fall away from my holy purpose.

1. Ps. lxxxvi, 4.　　　2. Luke xix, 9.　　　3. Matt. xv, 32.

Man's senses are prone to evil from his youth up,[1] and without the aid of this divine remedy he soon lapses into yet greater wickedness. Holy Communion both restrains a man from evil, and establishes him in goodness. For if I am so often careless and lukewarm now when I celebrate or communicate, what would become of me were I to neglect this remedy, or fail to seek this most powerful aid? And although I am neither fit nor rightly disposed to celebrate daily, yet I will endeavour at proper times to receive Your divine Mysteries, and present myself to receive this great grace. For this is the chief comfort of the faithful soul, as long as she dwells afar from You in this mortal body, that ever mindful of her God, she may often devoutly receive her Beloved.

O Lord God, Creator and Giver of life to all souls, how wonderful is Your kindness and mercy to us, that You should stoop to visit the poor and humble soul, and to satisfy her hunger with Your whole Divinity and Humanity! Happy the mind and blessed the soul that deserves to receive You with devotion, and in receiving You, to be filled with spiritual joy! How great a Lord does the soul receive! How beloved the Guest she welcomes! How delightful the Companion she invites to enter! How faithful the Friend she makes! How gracious and noble the Spouse she embraces – one to be loved and desired above all others! O dear and most beloved Lord, let Heaven and earth in all their beauty keep silence before You; for whatever of praise and beauty they possess comes from Your generous goodness. They cannot approach the beauty of Your Name, and Your Wisdom is infinite.[2]

1. Gen. viii, 21.   2. Ps. cxlvii, 5.

CHAPTER 4

On the Many Blessings Granted to the Devout Communicant

THE DISCIPLE. O Lord my God, so direct Your servant with the blessings of Your goodness,[1] that I may worthily and devoutly approach Your glorious Sacrament. Stir up my heart to seek You, and rouse me from sleep and sloth. Visit me with Your salvation,[2] that my spirit may taste Your sweetness, which in this Sacrament lies richly concealed, as in a fountain. Give me light to reverence this great Mystery: give me strength, to believe with unshakeable faith. For this is Your work, and it is not within the power of man; it is by Your sacred institution, and not an invention of men. No one of himself is capable of grasping and understanding these things, which are beyond even the high knowledge of the Angels. How then shall I, an unworthy sinner, mere dust and ashes, search out and understand so deep and sacred a mystery?

Lord, in simplicity of heart,[3] in firm good faith, and at Your bidding, I approach You with hope and reverence. I firmly believe that You are truly present in this Sacrament, both God and Man. It is Your desire that I should receive You, and be united to You in love. Therefore, I implore Your mercy, and beg You to give me an especial grace, that I may wholly melt and overflow with love for You, and that henceforward I may seek no consolation but Yourself. For this most high and venerable Sacrament is the health of soul and body, the cure of every spiritual malady. By it, our vices are cured, our passions restrained, temptations are lessened, grace is given in fuller measure, and virtue once established is fostered; faith is confirmed, hope is strengthened, and love kindled and deepened.

1. Ps. xxi, 3.   2. Ps. cvi, 4.   3. 1 Chron. xxix, 17.

O my God, Guardian of the soul, Restorer of man's weakness, and Giver of every spiritual consolation, You have given, and still often give many blessings in this Sacrament to Your beloved servants who receive You with devotion. Great are the comforts that You bestow on men in their many troubles, raising them from the depths of dejection to hope in Your protection. You restore and enlighten them with fresh graces, so that those who before Communion were distraught and without devotion, find themselves changed for the better after the refreshment of this heavenly Food and Drink. You do this for Your loved ones of set purpose, that they may truly know and patiently experience their own weakness, and what blessings of grace they receive from You; for of themselves they are cold, dry, and indifferent; but through You they become fervent, eager, and devout. Shall not any who approach the Fount of sweetness with humility carry away some of its sweetness with them? Or shall not any who stand close to a great fire enjoy some of its heat? And You, Lord, are the Fountain, ever full and overflowing; You are the ever-burning Fire that can never be extinguished.

Therefore, if I may not draw from the fullness of the Fountain,[1] nor fully quench my thirst, I will yet place my lips to this heavenly Spring, and receive some drops to allay my thirst. And although I may not become altogether heavenly and ardent like the Cherubim and Seraphim, yet I will give myself to devotion and prepare my heart, that I may at least obtain a portion of the divine fire by humbly receiving this life-giving Sacrament. O good Jesus, most holy Saviour, I pray You of Your mercy and grace to supply whatever is lacking in me; for You deign to call men to You saying, 'Come to Me, all who labour and are heavy laden, and I will refresh you.'

1. Isa. xii, 3.

193

I labour in the sweat of my brow;[1] I am tortured by grief of heart; I am burdened by my sins, troubled by temptations, entangled and oppressed by many evil passions. There is none who can help, none who can liberate and save, but You, O Lord God, my Saviour: to You, then, I commit myself and all I have, that You may guard and guide me to eternal life. Receive me for the praise and glory of Your Name, who have given Your Body and Blood to be my food and drink. O Lord God, my Saviour, grant that through the reception of Your Mysteries, the fire of devotion may kindle in me.

CHAPTER 5

On the Dignity of the Sacrament, and of the Priestly Office

CHRIST. Had you the purity of the Angels, and the holiness of Saint John the Baptist, you would still be unworthy to receive or touch this Sacrament. For it is not due to any merit of his own that a man is allowed to consecrate and handle the Sacrament of Christ, and receive the Bread of Angels[2] as his food. High the office, and great the dignity of a priest, to whom is granted what is not granted to Angels; for only a rightly ordained priest has power to celebrate the Eucharist and to hallow the Body of Christ. The priest is the minister of God, using the words of God by His own command and appointment: but God Himself is the principal agent and unseen worker, to whose will all things are subject,[3] and whose command all creatures obey.

In all that relates to this sublime Sacrament, you should have regard to God's word, rather than your own senses or any visible sign. Therefore, when you approach the Altar, let it be with awe and reverence. Consider from whom this

1. Gen. iii, 19.   2. Ps. lxxviii, 26.   3. Wisd. xii, 18.

ministry proceeds, that has been delivered to you by the imposition of the Bishop's hands.[1] You have been made a priest, and ordained to celebrate the Sacrament: see, then, that you offer this sacrifice to God faithfully, regularly, and devoutly, and that your life is blameless.[2] Your obligations are now greater; you are bound to exercise stricter self-discipline, and to aim at a higher degree of holiness. A priest should be adorned with all virtues, and show an example of holy life to others.[3] His life should not be like that of worldly men, but like that of the Angels,[4] or of perfect men on earth.

A priest clothed in sacred vestments occupies the place of Christ, that he may humbly intercede with God for himself and for all men.[5] He wears the sign of the Cross both before and behind him, that he may be ever mindful of His Lord's Passion. He wears the Cross before him on his chasuble, that he may diligently observe the footsteps of Christ, and earnestly study to follow them.[6] His shoulders also are signed with the Cross, that he may in mercy and for the love of God bear every injury done him by others. He wears the Cross before him, that he may grieve for his own sins; behind him, that he may compassionately lament the sins of others, ever mindful that he is appointed a mediator between God and the sinner, and that he may not cease from prayer and the Holy Sacrifice until he deserve to win grace and mercy. And when a priest celebrates the Eucharist, he honours God, and gives joy to the Angels; he edifies the Church, helps the living, obtains rest for the departed, and makes himself a sharer in all good things.

1. 1 Tim. iv, 14.   3. Titus ii, 7.   5. Heb. v, 3; vii, 27.
2. 1 Tim. iii, 2; 2 Pet.   4. Phil. iii, 20.   6. 1 Pet. ii, 21.
    iii, 14.

CHAPTER 6
On Preparation for Communion

THE DISCIPLE. Lord, when I consider Your dignity and my own wretchedness, I am full of fear and confusion. For if I do not receive You, I refuse life; and if I intrude myself unworthily, I incur Your displeasure. What, then, shall I do, my God, my Helper, my Counsellor in need? Show me the right way, and set before me some short exercise, suitable for Holy Communion. I must learn to prepare my heart for You devoutly and reverently, both for the fruitful receiving of Your Sacrament, and for the right offering of so august and divine a Sacrifice.

CHAPTER 7
On Self-Examination, and the Purpose of Amendment

CHRIST. It is fitting that a priest be endowed above all else with humility of heart and profound reverence, and that when he celebrates, handles or receives this Sacrament, he does so with firm faith and with the sacred purpose of giving glory to God. Therefore carefully examine your conscience to the best of your ability, cleansing and purifying it by true contrition and humble confession. Thus will you retain no grave matter on it that may keep you from approaching the Sacrament. Grieve for your sins in general, and for your besetting sins in particular. And, if time allow, confess to God from the depths of your heart all the misery of your passions.[1]

Grieve that you are still so carnal and worldly; so un-disciplined in your passions, and so full of bodily cravings; so unguarded in your outward sense; so often engrossed in vain

1. Ps. xxxii, 5.

fancies; so absorbed in worldly affairs and so indifferent to spiritual; so easily moved to laughter and levity, so disinclined to sorrow and penitence; so eager for ease and self-indulgence, so averse to zeal and self-discipline; so anxious to hear news and see fine sights, so reluctant to accept humble and simple things; so greedy for great possessions, so miserly in giving, so tenacious in keeping; so intemperate in speech, so unwilling to keep silence; so disorderly in manners, so impetuous in action; so greedy for food, so deaf to the Word of God; so quick to rest, so slow to work; so wide-awake to listen to idle tales, so sleepy at holy vigils; so hurried in your devotions, so wandering in attention; so careless in reciting the Hours, so lukewarm at the Eucharist, so lacking in devotion at Communion; so easily distracted, so seldom wholly recollected; so suddenly roused to anger, so quick to take offence; so ready to judge, so severe in reproof; so cheerful in prosperity, so weak in adversity; so frequently proposing many good deeds, and so seldom doing them.

When you have confessed and grieved over these and your other faults with deep sorrow and contrition at your own weakness, make a firm resolve to amend your life and to advance in holiness. Then surrender yourself and your will entirely to Me, and offer yourself on the altar of your heart as a perpetual sacrifice to the honour of My Name. Faithfully commit yourself to Me, body and soul, that you may worthily approach and offer this Sacrifice to God, and receive the Sacrament of My Body to the health of your soul.

There is no more worthy offering nor fuller satisfaction for the cleansing of sins than to offer one's self wholly and purely to God, together with the offering of the Body of Christ in the Eucharist and in Communion. When a man is truly penitent and does his best, then whenever he comes to Me for pardon and grace, I will remember his sins no more, but will forgive them all. 'I live,' says the Lord, 'and do not desire the death of a sinner, but rather that he be converted and live.'[1]

CHAPTER 8
On the Offering of Christ on the Cross

CHRIST. Naked I hung on the Cross with arms outstretched, offering Myself freely to God the Father for your sins,[2] My whole Person a sacrifice of divine propitiation: you, too, must willingly offer yourself daily to Me in the Eucharist with all your powers and affections as a pure and holy offering. I require nothing less of you than that you should strive to yield yourself wholly to Me. Whatever you offer to Me besides yourself, I account as nothing; I seek not your gift, but yourself.[3]

Were you to possess everything in the world except Me, it could not satisfy you; so neither can anything you give Me be acceptable without the gift of yourself. Offer yourself to Me, and give yourself wholly to God; so shall your offering be acceptable.[4] I offered Myself wholly to the Father for you: I have given My very Body and Blood to be your food, that I may be all yours, and that you may be mine for ever. But if you trust in yourself, and do not offer yourself freely to My will, your offering is not complete, nor can our union be perfect. A free offering of yourself into the hands of God must therefore precede all your doings if you desire to obtain freedom and grace. The reason why so few receive inward light and freedom is that they cannot

1. Ezek. xviii, 22; Isa.   2. Isa. liii, 7; Heb. ix,   3. Phil. iv, 17.
   xliii, 25; Heb. x,17.   28.   4. Ecclus. xxxv, 7.

wholly renounce self. My words remain unalterable: who-
ever does not renounce everything cannot be My disciple.[1]
Therefore if you wish to be My disciple, offer yourself to
Me with all your heart.

CHAPTER 9

How we must Offer Ourselves wholly to God and
Pray for all Men

THE DISCIPLE. Lord, all things in Heaven and earth are
Yours.[2] I desire to give myself to You as a free offering, and
to be Yours for ever. O Lord, in simplicity of heart I offer
myself to You this day, to be Your servant for ever:[3] I do
this as an act of homage to You, and as an act of perpetual
praise. Accept me, together with the Holy Sacrifice of Your
precious Body which I plead before You this day in the
unseen presence of adoring Angels, that it may avail to my
salvation and that of all Your people.

Lord, I offer on Your altar of reconciliation all the sins and
offences that I have ever committed before You and Your
holy Angels, from the day of my first sin until now, praying
You to burn and consume them all in the fire of Your love.
Blot out the stains of my sins, and cleanse my conscience[4]
from all offences: restore the grace lost by my sin: grant me
full forgiveness, and of Your mercy receive me with the kiss
of peace.

What can I do to atone for my sins, but humbly confess
and lament them, and constantly implore Your propitiation?
Hear me, I beg, in Your mercy, as I stand before You, O my
God. All my sins are utterly hateful to me, and I resolve
never to commit them again: I am sorry for them, and will

1. Luke xiv, 33.   3. 1 Chron. xxix, 17.
2. 1 Chron. xxix, 11.   4. Heb. ix. 14; 1 John i, 7.

grieve for them as long as I live. I am ready to do penance, and to make any amends in my power. Forgive me, O God, forgive me for Your holy Name's sake,[1] and save my soul, that You have redeemed by Your precious Blood.[2] I commit myself entirely to Your mercy, and resign myself into Your hands; deal with me according to Your goodness, and not as my malice and wickedness deserves.[3]

I offer to You also whatever is good in me, though it be little and imperfect, that You may strengthen and hallow it, make it dear and acceptable to You, and raise it continually towards perfection. And bring me, stubborn and unprofitable servant as I am, to a worthy and blessed end.

I offer You also all the holy aspirations of devout persons; the needs of my parents, friends, brothers, sisters, and all who are dear to me; and the needs of all who have desired or asked me to pray and offer the Eucharist for them and theirs, whether living or departed. I pray that all these may enjoy the assistance of Your grace, the aid of Your comfort, protection from dangers, and deliverance from pains to come; and that, freed from all evils, they may offer glad praise and thanks to You.

I offer You also my prayers and the Sacrifice of Peace in particular for those who have in any way injured, grieved or maligned me, or who have done me any kind of harm or hurt; likewise for any whom I have at any time grieved, troubled, injured or offended by word or deed, knowingly or unknowingly; that You may in mercy pardon all our sins and offences one against another. O Lord, take from our hearts all suspicion, ill-feeling, anger, and contention, and whatever may injure charity and brotherly love. Have mercy, O Lord, have mercy on all who ask Your mercy.[4]

1. Ps. xxv, 11.   3. 1 Macc. xiii, 46.
2. 1 Pet. i, 19.   4. Ps. cxxiii, 3.

Give grace to those who sorely need it; and help us all so to live that we may worthily enjoy Your grace, and finally come to everlasting life.

CHAPTER 10

That Holy Communion is not to be Lightly Foregone

CHRIST. Come regularly to the Fountain of grace and divine mercy, the Fountain of goodness and all purity, that you may be healed of your passions and vices, and be rendered more vigilant and strong to resist all the temptations and deceits of the devil. For your old Enemy knows well the abundant fruit and powerful remedy contained in Holy Communion, and tries by every means in his power to discourage and prevent the faithful and devout from receiving it.

Satan's most violent assaults often come upon people whenever they make their preparation for Holy Communion. As it is written in Job, that wicked spirit comes among the children of God[1] to trouble them with his accustomed malice, or to make them fearful and uncertain. In this way he seeks to lessen their love for God, or to destroy their faith, that they may perhaps entirely abandon Communion, or come to it with little devotion. But pay no regard to his snares and cunning illusions, however vile and horrible, and hurl back these fantasies on his own head. Treat the Evil One with the contempt and mockery that he deserves, and never abandon Holy Communion on account of his insults and disturbances.

People are often hindered by an undue concern about devout feelings, and by anxieties about confession. In such cases, follow the advice of a wise director, and lay aside all

1. Job i, 7.

scruple, for it is an obstacle to the grace of God, and destroys all devotion of the mind. Do not postpone receiving Communion for every little worry and doubt, but go at once to confession, and willingly forgive all who have done you ill and if you have done ill to anyone, humbly ask pardon, and God will gladly forgive you.[1]

Of what use is it to delay confession, or to put off Holy Communion? Cleanse yourself at once; spit out the poison quickly, and take the remedy without hesitation; swift action will aid you better than delay. If for some reason you put it off today, tomorrow some greater evil may befall you; in this way you may be kept from Communion a long while, and become more unfit than ever. Therefore shake off your present sloth and dullness as quickly as possible, for it is no advantage to remain a long time in disquiet and distress, nor to absent yourself from the sacred mysteries on account of your everyday difficulties. On the contrary, it is very hurtful to delay Communion over a long period, for this often results in sloth and spiritual dryness.

Some half-hearted and careless people, alas, readily seize on any excuse to postpone their confession, and desire on that account to defer their sacred Communion, unwilling that they should be obliged to keep a stricter watch on their lives. How small the love and feeble the devotion of those who so lightly put off holy Communion! Happy the man, and dear to God, who so keeps his heart and life pure, that he would be eager and well prepared to communicate daily if it were possible, and if he might do it without appearing remarkable. He who sometimes abstains out of humility, or is legitimately prevented, is to be commended for his reverence. But if sloth has crept upon him, he must rouse himself with all his energy, and God will strengthen his

1. Matt. v, 23; vi, 12.

desire for the sake of his good intent, which He regards with especial favour.

Whenever anyone is unavoidably prevented, then so long as he preserves a good will and holy desire for Communion, he will not lose the benefits of the Sacrament. For anyone who sincerely desires it may on any day and at any hour make unhindered a Spiritual Communion with Christ to the health of his soul. None the less, on certain Feasts and at certain Seasons he ought to receive the Body of his Redeemer sacramentally with love and reverence, and seek the honour and praise of God before his own consolation. For as often as anyone receives mystic communion and spiritual refreshment, he recalls with devotion the mystery of the Incarnation and Passion of Christ, and is roused anew to love of Him. But he who prepares himself only at the approach of a Festival, or when custom prescribes it, will often be entirely unprepared.

Blessed is the man who, whenever he celebrates the Eucharist or receives Communion, offers himself to Our Lord as a living sacrifice. And when celebrating, be neither too slow nor too hurried, but observe the common usage of those with whom you are living. Be careful not to cause irritation or weariness to others, but observe the customs appointed by the Fathers, and consider the benefit of others before your personal devotion or preference.

How the Body of Christ and the Holy Scriptures are most Necessary to the Faithful Soul

THE DISCIPLE. Dearest Lord Jesus, how great is the joy of the devout soul who feasts at Your banquet, where the food set before it is none other than Your very Self, its only-Beloved, desirable above all the heart's desire! How deeply I long to pour out my heartfelt tears in Your presence, and like the devoted Magdalen, bathe Your feet with my tears.[1] But where is my devotion? And where this flood of holy tears? Surely, in Your presence and that of Your holy Angels my whole heart should burn and melt for joy! For here You are truly present with me in Your Sacrament, though veiled beneath another form.

I could not endure to gaze on You in the full glory of Your Divinity, nor could the whole world bear the splendour and glory of Your Majesty. Therefore You bear with my frailty, and conceal Yourself in this holy Sacrament. Here I truly possess and adore Him whom the Angels adore in Heaven;[2] I, as yet, by faith alone, but they by sight and unconcealed.[3] I must rest content with the light of true faith, and so remain until the day of endless glory dawn, and the shadow of figures pass away.[4] When that which is perfect is come,[5] the use of Sacraments will come to an end, for the Blessed in glory need no sacramental healing. They enjoy the presence of God for ever, and view his unveiled glory;[6] transformed from glory[7] into glory of His own unsearchable divinity, they taste the Word of God made man, as He[8] was from the beginning, and as He abides eternally.[9]

1. Luke vii, 38: John xii, 3.
2. Heb. i, 6.
3. 2 Cor. v, 7.
4. Song of Solomon, ii, 17.
5. 1 Cor. xiii, 10.
6. 1 Cor. xiii, 12.
7. 2 Cor. iii, 18.
8. John i, 14.
9. 1 Pet. i, 25.

When I consider these wonders, even spiritual consolations become wearisome, for so long as I cannot see my Lord in His unveiled glory, I value as nothing all that I can see or hear in this world. Lord, You are my witness[1] that nothing can comfort me, nor can I rest content in anything created, but in You alone, O my God, on whom I long to gaze for ever. But this is not possible for me in this mortal life, so I must cultivate true patience, and submit all my desires to You. Your holy Saints, who now share Your joy in the Kingdom of Heaven, during their lives waited the coming of Your glory with great faith and patience.[2] What they believed, I also believe; what they hoped to enjoy, I hope to enjoy; and whither they have arrived, by Your grace, I hope to arrive also. Meanwhile I will walk in faith, strengthened by the example of the Saints; the holy scriptures shall be the comfort and mirror of my life, and above all Your most holy Body shall be my especial remedy and refuge.

I now realize that there are two things especially necessary to me, without which this life of sorrow would be unbearable. While in the prison-house of this body, I acknowledge my need of two things – food and light. You have therefore given me in my weakness Your sacred Body to be the refreshment of my soul and body, and have set Your Word as a lamp to my feet.[3] Without these two, I cannot rightly live; for the Word of God is the light of my soul, and Your Sacrament is the bread of my life.[4] One might describe them as two tables, set on either side in the treasury of holy Church. The one is the table of the holy altar, having on it the holy bread,[5] the precious Body of Christ; the other is that of the divine law, that enshrines the holy doctrine, teaches the true faith, and unerringly guides

1. Rom. i, 9.   3. Ps. cxix, 105.   5. 1 Sam, xxi, 4.
2. Heb. vi, 12.   4. John vi, 35.

our steps even within the veil[1] that guards the Holy of Holies.

O Lord Jesus, Light eternal, I thank You for the table of holy teaching that You have given us through Your servants the Prophets, Apostles, and other teachers.[2] O Creator and Redeemer of men, in order to manifest to the whole world the depths of Your love, You have prepared a great Supper,[3] at which You offer us, not the Lamb of the old Law, but Your own most holy Body and Blood to be our food. In this sacred Feast, You give joy to all the faithful, granting them to drink deeply from the Cup of Salvation,[4] which holds all the joys of Heaven, while the holy Angels share the feast with us, but with even deeper delight.

Oh, how high and honourable is the office of priests, to whom is given power to consecrate with sacred words the Lord of majesty, to bless Him with their lips, to hold Him in their hands, to receive Him in their mouths, and to communicate Him to others. How clean should be the hands, how pure the lips, how holy the body, how spotless the heart of a priest, into whom the Author of all purity so often enters. From the mouth of a priest, who so often receives the Sacrament of Christ, nothing should issue but what is holy, true, and edifying. Let his eyes, that so often look on the Body of Christ, be simple and chaste. Let his hands, that handle the Creator of Heaven and earth, be pure and raised to Heaven.[5] For to priests in particular are addressed the words of the Law, 'Be holy, for I the Lord your God am holy.'[6]

Almighty God, let Your grace assist us, that we who have undertaken the office of priesthood may be enabled to serve You worthily and devoutly in all purity and with a good conscience. And although we cannot remain in such inno-

1. Heb. vi, 19; ix, 3.   3. Luke xiv, 16.   5. 1 Tim. ii, 8.
2. Eph. iv, 11.   4. Ps. xxiii, 5.   6. Lev. xix, 2.

cency of life as we ought, yet grant us sincerely to lament our sins, and to serve You henceforward with greater devotion, in the spirit of humility and with good will and intention.

CHAPTER 12

On the Need for Careful Preparation to Receive Christ in Holy Communion

CHRIST. I am the lover of purity and giver of all holiness. I seek a pure heart, and there will I dwell.[1] Prepare and make ready for Me a large upper room, and there will I and My disciples eat the Passover[2] with you. If you wish Me to come and dwell with you, purify the old leaven,[3] and cleanse the dwelling of your heart. Exclude the whole world and its sinful clamour; sit there alone, like a sparrow on the roof-top,[4] and consider your sinfulness in bitterness of soul.[5] For every loving person prepares the best and fairest room for his dear friend, and in doing so, shows his affection.

However, know that even your best efforts cannot make a worthy preparation for Me, although you were to prepare for a whole year and do nothing else beside. It is of My mercy and grace alone that you are allowed to approach My table; as though a beggar were invited to a rich man's supper, and could offer no return for his kindness save humble gratitude.[6] Do whatever lies in your power, and do it earnestly, not out of habit or necessity, but with awe and reverent love receive the Body of your Lord and God, who deigns to come to you. It is My invitation and My bidding: I will supply whatever is lacking in you. Come, therefore, and receive Me.

When I grant you the grace of devotion, give thanks to

1. Acts vii, 49 : Isa. lxvi, 1.
2. Mark xiv, 15 ; Luke xxii, 12.
3. 1 Cor. v, 7.
4. Ps. cii, 7.
5. Isa. xxxviii, 15.
6. Luke xiv, 12.

God, not because you deserve to enjoy it, but because I have had mercy on you. And if you feel no devotion, but suffer dryness of soul, persevere in prayer, sigh, and knock;[1] persist until you merit to receive some crumb or drop of saving grace. You have need of Me; I have no need of you.[2] You do not come to sanctify Me, but I come to sanctify and raise you. You come in order to be hallowed and united to Me; that you may receive fresh grace, and be inspired anew to amendment of life. Do not neglect this grace,[3] but prepare yourself with all care, and invite your Beloved into your heart.

Not only must you make a devout preparation before Holy Communion, but also carefully foster your devotion after receiving the Sacrament. No less vigilance is required after Communion than devout preparation beforehand. For a constant vigilance after Communion is the best preparation for receiving richer graces; and a man will be entirely undisposed to do this if he straightway turns to outward pleasures. Beware of much talk:[4] remain in some quiet place, and savour the presence of God; for you possess Him whom the whole world cannot take away from you. I am He to whom you should offer your whole self, that, set free from care, you may no longer live in yourself, but in Me.[5]

1. Matt. vii, 7: Luke   2. 2 Macc. xiv, 35.   4. Prov. x, 19.
xi, 9.   3. 1 Tim. iv, 14.   5. John xv, 4; Gal. ii, 20.

CHAPTER 13

How the Devout Soul should Sincerely Desire
Union with Christ in his Sacrament

THE DISCIPLE. Lord, who will grant me to find You alone, to open my whole heart to You, and to enjoy You as my soul desires, that none may henceforward despise me, nor any creature disturb or notice me; that You alone may speak to me, and I to You, as a lover speaks to his beloved, and as friend to friend?[1] For this is my prayer and desire, that I may be wholly united to You, and withdraw my heart from all created things; that through Holy Communion and frequent offering of the Eucharist, I may come to delight in heavenly and eternal things more and more. O my Lord and God, when shall I be wholly united to and absorbed into You, and wholly unmindful of myself? You in me, and I in You:[2] so grant us to abide in one for ever.

You are indeed my Beloved, preferred before thousands,[3] in whom my soul delights to dwell all the days of my life. You are the Giver of true peace, in whom is perfect peace and true rest, and outside of whom is toil and sorrow without end. You are the true and hidden God,[4] whose dealings are not with the wicked, but with the humble and simple.[5] How sweet is Your Spirit, O Lord, who to show Your graciousness to Your children, refresh them with the most sweet Bread that comes down from Heaven.[6] There is no nation, however great, whose gods dwell so near to it[7] as You, our God, who are present to all Your faithful, to whom, for their daily comfort and elevation of their heart You give Yourself as food and delight.

1. Exod. xxxiii, 11.
2. John xvii, 21.
3. Song of Solomon v, 10.
4. Prov. iii, 33.
5. Isa. xlv, 15.
6. Wisd. xvi, 20.
7. Deut. iv, 7.

What other people is so favoured as the Christian people?
Or what creature under heaven is so beloved as the devout
soul, into whom God enters, nourishing it with His glorious
Body? O unspeakable grace, O marvellous condescension,
O boundless love, bestowed on mankind alone! But what
return can I make to the Lord[1] for all His grace and overflowing love? Nothing that I can give will be more acceptable to Him than my whole heart, to be inwardly united to
Him in utter surrender. When my soul is perfectly united to
God, my whole being will be filled with joy. Then will He
say to me, 'If you will dwell with Me, I will dwell with you'
and I shall answer Him, 'Lord, dwell with me, I pray, for I
will gladly remain with You. It is my sole desire, that my
heart be united to You.'

CHAPTER 14
On Ardent Desire for the Body of Christ

DISCIPLE. Lord, how boundless is Your goodness, which You
reserve for those who love You![2] When I think of some
devout Christians who frequent Your Sacrament with the
greatest devotion and love, I feel ashamed and confounded
that I approach Your Altar and the table of Holy Communion with so tepid and cold a heart; that I remain so dry
and lacking in love; that my heart remains unkindled in
Your presence, O God; neither am I so strongly drawn nor
lovingly disposed as many devout folk. For these, out of
their ardent desire for Communion and heartfelt love for
You, could not restrain their tears, but from the very depth
of their souls longed both with heart and body for You, O
God, the living Fountain.[3] In no other way could they

1. Ps. cxvi, 12.　　2. Ps. xxxi, 21.　　3. Jer. ii, 13; Ps. xlii, 2; Rev. vii, 17.

appease or satisfy their hunger, but by receiving Your Body with all joy and eagerness of spirit.

O, how true was their burning faith – in itself a true and evident token of Your divine Presence! For they truly know their Lord in the Breaking of Bread, whose hearts burn so ardently when Jesus walks with them.[1] Alas, such devotion and affection, such unfeigned love and fervour is seldom felt by me. O good and kind Jesus, have mercy on me, and grant me Your poor mendicant at least sometimes to feel a measure of this heartfelt desire of Your love in sacred Communion, that my faith may be strengthened; that my hope in Your goodness may be fostered; and that love once perfectly kindled, having tasted the Bread of Heaven, may never fail. Your mercy, O Lord, is boundless enough to grant me even this favour from which I long; and when it shall please You, I pray You of Your grace and generosity to visit me with the spirit of fervour. For though I do not burn with so ardent a desire as those who are so supremely devoted to You, yet by Your grace I do long to have that great and burning desire: and I beg and pray that I may have part with all Your true lovers, and be numbered in their holy company.

CHAPTER 15
How Devotion is Won by Humility and Self-Denial

CHRIST. You must seek the grace of devotion with earnestness, ask for it with real desire, wait for it with patience and trust, receive it with thankfulness, keep it with humility, use it with diligence, and commit to God the time and manner of His heavenly gift. Above all, humble yourself when you feel little or no inner devotion, and do not be too depressed

1. Luke xxiv, 32.

or discouraged, for God often grants in one short moment what He has withheld for a long while. And sometimes He grants in due time what He delayed to grant at your first request.

Were grace always granted at once and to be had for the asking, the weakness of man could hardly support it. The grace of devotion must therefore be awaited with firm hope and humble patience. When it is not granted, or when it is withdrawn, regard this as due to yourself and your own sinfulness. Sometimes it is a small matter that hinders or conceals grace – if, indeed, it may be termed a small thing and not grave that delays so great a good. But once you have removed this obstacle, whether small or great, and have perfectly overcome it, you shall have your desire.

As soon as you shall yield yourself to God with all your heart, and seek nothing for your own will and pleasure, but place yourself without reserve at His disposal, you shall find yourself united to Him, and at peace. Nothing will afford you more joy and satisfaction than the perfect fulfilling of God's will. Whoever, therefore, raises his intent to God with a pure heart, and disengages himself from all inordinate love or hatred of any creature, shall best be prepared to receive grace, and be worthy of the gift of devotion. For Our Lord bestows His blessings where He finds vessels empty to receive them. And the more completely a man renounces worldly things, and the more perfectly he dies to self by the conquest of self, the sooner will grace be given, the more richly will it be infused, and the nearer to God will it raise the heart set free from the world.

Such a person will overflow and wonder, and his heart will be enlarged within him,[1] for the hand of the Lord is upon him, and he has placed himself wholly in His hand for ever. Thus shall the man be blessed who seeks God with his whole

1. Isa. lx, 5.

heart;[1] he has not received his soul in vain. When he receives the sacred Eucharist, he merits the great grace of divine union, for he does not look to his own devotion and comfort, but beyond all such devotion and comfort he seeks the honour and glory of God.

CHAPTER 16

How we should Declare our Needs to Christ, and Ask his Grace

THE DISCIPLE. Most dear and loving Lord, whom I now desire to receive with all devotion. You know my weakness and my many needs, the countless sins and vices that afflict me, and how often I am discouraged, tempted, troubled, and defiled. I come to You for healing; I beg You to comfort and relieve me. I make my prayer to Him who knows all things,[2] to whom my inmost thoughts lie unconcealed, and who alone can perfectly comfort and aid me. You know the graces I most need, and how lacking I am in all virtues.

See, Lord, I stand before You naked and poor, begging for grace and imploring mercy. Appease the hunger of this, Your beggar; warm my coldness by the fire of Your love, and lighten my blindness by the light of Your presence. Turn for me all worldly things into bitterness, all grievous and harmful things into patience, and cause me to despise and put out of mind all base and material things. Raise my heart to You in Heaven, and let me no longer be a wanderer on the face of the earth. Be my sole delight henceforward and for ever, for You alone are my food and drink, my love and my joy, my delight and my supreme good.

Oh, that You would set me wholly afire by Your presence, and change me into Yourself, that I might be made one

1. Ps. cxix, 2.   2. John xxi, 17.

spirit with You[1] by the grace of inward vision, and by the fusion of ardent love. Do not send me away hungry and thirsty, but deal with me in Your mercy, as You have dealt so marvellously with Your Saints. How wonderful it would be, were I wholly on fire with You and dead to self, for You, O Lord, are the Fire unquenchable[2] that burns for ever; You are the Love that purifies the heart and lights the mind.

CHAPTER 17

On Ardent Love and Eager Desire to Receive Christ

THE DISCIPLE. Dear Lord, I long to receive You with deepest devotion and ardent love, and with all the affection and favour of my heart, as many Saints and holy persons have longed to receive You in Communion, who were especially pleasing to You by the holiness of their lives, and were on fire with devotion. O my God, Eternal Love, my supreme good and eternal delight, I wish to receive You with the most eager devotion and deepest reverence that any of Your Saints have ever felt, or could feel.

Although I am not fit to enjoy such feelings of devotion as they, yet I offer You all the love in my heart, as though I alone were moved by these most fitting and ardent longings. So, whatever a pious heart can conceive or desire, that I offer You with all reverence and love. I wish to withhold no part of myself, but freely and most gladly to make an offering to You of all that I am or have. O Lord my God, my Creator and Redeemer, I wish to receive You today with that affection, reverence, praise and honour, with that gratitude, worthiness, and love, with that faith, hope, and purity with which Your most holy Mother, the glorious Virgin Mary, desired and received You, when she devoutly

1. 1 Cor. vi, 17.   2. Lev. vi, 13.

and humbly answered the Angel who brought the joyful message of the Mystery of the Incarnation: 'Behold, the handmaid of the Lord: be it done to me according to Your word.'[1]

And as Your blessed herald John the Baptist, greatest among the Saints, who was glad and leaped for joy[2] of the Holy Spirit while yet in his mother's womb, and who, when he later saw Jesus walking among men,[3] devoutly and lovingly humbled himself, saying 'The friend of the Bridegroom, who stands and hears Him, is glad because of the Bridegroom's voice.'[4] Like these, I too wish to be afire with great and holy desires, and to offer myself to You with all my heart. I also offer and present before You the praises, the glowing affections, the raptures, the supernatural revelations and heavenly visions of all devout hearts, together with all the virtues and praises that are or ever shall be offered by all creatures in Heaven or on earth. I plead them for myself, and for all who have been commended to my prayers, that You may be worthily praised and glorified for ever.

Accept, O Lord my God, my vows and my desire to offer You infinite praise and boundless blessing; for these are Your rightful due, by reason of Your unspeakable greatness.[5] These I render, and wish to render every day and every moment of time; and I lovingly pray and entreat all the heavenly host to join with me and all the faithful in offering You praise and thanksgiving.

Let all people, tribes and tongues[6] praise and exalt Your sweet and holy Name with great joy and fervent devotion. And may all who reverently and devoutly celebrate Your sublime Sacrament, and receive It with full faith, merit to obtain Your grace and mercy, humbly interceding for me, a

1. Luke i, 38.　　3. John i, 36.　　5. Ps. cl, 2.
2. Luke i, 44.　　4. John iii, 29.　　6. Rev. vii, 9.

sinner. And when they shall have obtained the devotion they desire, and blissful union with Yourself, and have left Your sacred and heavenly Table truly comforted and marvellously refreshed, let them, I pray, remember me, who am so poor.

CHAPTER 18

How we should Approach Christ's Sacrament Humbly, Submitting Reason to Holy Faith

CHRIST. Beware of curious and unprofitable inquiry into the Myseries of this most holy Sacrament, if you would avoid being plunged into the depths of doubt; for those who attempt to search into the majesty of God will be overwhelmed with its glory.[1] God can do more than man is able to comprehend; yet we may humbly and reverently search for truth, so long as the seeker is always willing to be taught, and to follow the sound teachings of the Fathers.

Blessed is that simplicity which rejects obscure inquiry and advances along the sure and open road of God's Commandments.[2] Many have lost their devotion by attempting to pry into matters too high for them. It is faith and a holy life that are required of you, not a lofty intellect or knowledge of the profound mysteries of God. For if you cannot understand or grasp things that are beneath you, how will you comprehend those that are above you? Therefore submit yourself to God, and humble your reason to faith, and the light of knowledge shall be granted you in so far as it be profitable and necessary.

Some are sorely tempted about faith and the Sacraments, but this is due to the Devil rather than to themselves. Do not be anxious; do not fight your thoughts, or attempt to answer any doubts that the Devil suggests: trust in God's

1. Prov. xxv, 27.   2. Ps. cxix, 35.

word, believe His Saints and Prophets, and the wicked
enemy will flee from you.[1] Often it is very profitable that
the servant of God should experience such doubts, since the
Devil does not tempt unbelievers and sinners who are
already his own; but he tempts and vexes the faithful and
devout in every way he can.

Go forward, then, with simple, undoubting faith, and
come to this Sacrament with humble reverence, confidently
committing to almighty God whatever you are not able to
understand. God never deceives; but man is deceived whenever he puts too much trust in himself. God walks with the
simple,[2] reveals Himself to the humble, gives understanding
to little ones, discloses His secrets to pure minds, and conceals His grace from the curious and conceited.[3]

All reason and natural research must follow faith, but not
precede or encroach on it. For in this most holy and excellent
Sacrament faith and love precede all else, working in ways
unknowable to man. The eternal God, transcendent and
infinite in power, works mightily and unsearchably[4] both in
heaven and earth,[5] nor can there be any searching out of His
wonders.[6] For were the works of God readily understand-
able by human reason, they would be neither wonderful nor
unspeakable.

1. James iv, 7.   3. Matt. xi, 25.   5. Ps. cxxxv, 6.
2. Ps. cxix, 130.   4. Job v, 9.   6. Isa. xl, 28.